THE NEW ORDEAL OF CHRISTIANITY

Paul Hutchinson

THE NEW ORDEAL
OF *Christianity*

ASSOCIATION PRESS

NEW YORK

THE NEW ORDEAL OF CHRISTIANITY

Copyright © 1957 by
National Board of Young Men's Christian Associations

Association Press, 291 Broadway, New York 7, N.Y.

Library of Congress catalog card number: 57-6887

55

Printed in the United States of America
American Book–Stratford Press, Inc., New York

Contents

Introduction

IN CONSIDERING "The New Ordeal of Christianity," it is not my purpose to analyze the nature of the crisis which confronts the churches in these times, or to sketch its extent. Others are doing that in a flood of books, magazine articles, radio and television broadcasts which never ceases flowing.

Nevertheless, the existence of this world crisis, this ordeal which Christianity must face, is something we cannot deny and cannot ignore. We all feel its influence —and in that word "all" I include every human being with full faculties, save perhaps a handful of primitive savages in the arid wastes of Australia—and even they are now being removed from their hidden villages in order to provide Great Britain with a proving ground for nuclear bombs—or other primitives in the Pygmy villages of the upper Congo or along the headwaters of the Amazon. Even such hitherto sealed-off regions as Tibet and Afghanistan find themselves penetrated and shaken by this upheaval in human affairs.

Whether this extraordinary period betokens the death of old orders of society—capitalism passing into eclipse in the West and feudalistic autocracy in the East—or whether we are writhing in the birth throes of some new order still struggling to be born, who can be sure? Perhaps both are taking place—both death *and* birth—since death may be a necessary forerunner of birth. The only thing of which we can be certain is that we are in the midst of a global crisis—a "time of troubles," to use Toynbee's phrase—which is agitating every region and every type of society and is affecting every phase of human activity.

We are warned by those whose words carry weight that this crisis differs from others which have gone before in that we now have at our command means for the extermination of our kind, while we have no assurance that our moral controls are strong enough to insure that these means will not be employed. Our technology has so far outstripped our morals that there is a real danger of racial self-destruction. Even if our native optimism rejects this terrifying prospect, we still know that we are caught in a time of awful tension and conflict, that we seem to be helpless puppets blindly stumbling about in a nightmare world where gigantic, impersonal forces which we cannot even comprehend, much less control, are locked in desperate battle. If Matthew Arnold, at the summit of the period when society was pervaded by what we commonly speak of as Victorian optimism, could say—

> ... we are here as on a darkling plain
> Swept with confused alarms of struggle and flight,
> Where ignorant armies clash by night—

how much more we in this hour? And this clash of ignorant armies by night will continue, we are forced to believe, throughout the lives of our children, and their children's children.

No, I am not attempting to establish the fact of the crisis or to analyze its nature. Rather, I wish to direct attention to a much more limited concern, but one which

seems to me of fundamental importance. The question
with which I shall try to deal is this: What is the relation of the Christian church to this crisis in human affairs? Or, since there is in objective fact no one Christian
church, What is the relation of the Christian churches
to the struggle in which man everywhere finds himself
involved? These Christian churches now circle the globe.
They are to be found on every continent. What contribution are they making to man's efforts to resolve the
contemporary crisis? And what contribution can they be
expected to make?

Most Christians, I assume, have believed that their
faith can and should be applied to every aspect of life.
I have given more than thirty years to editing a paper
which has, as a guiding rule for its selection of contents,
this conviction: "Religion (which to you and me must
mean Christianity) is responsible for the character of
civilization." You as Christians believe the same thing.
It is of the utmost importance, therefore, that we should
ask, *How is Christianity discharging this responsibility?
How are the churches, as the organized expression of
Christianity, measuring up to their task as guides in this
time of man's great need? To what extent are they revealing to befuddled and growingly desperate men the
nature of the crisis? To what extent are they modifying
or directing its outworking? In other words, how is Christianity facing this new ordeal? Or to what extent are the
churches being swept along like chips on history's flood?*

Properly to measure and assess the part being played
by the Christian churches of all kinds, on all continents,
would require at least a year of intensive research and
seminar discussion. Moreover, my knowledge is too limited to make possible a comprehensive survey. All I can
do is to skim rapidly over the surface of the present situ-

ation and hope that I may thereby awaken the interest of
professing Christians in pursuing more intensive and
more adequate study. The field is wide open; the materials are already immense and multiplying every month;
the importance of the inquiry for the future of man-
kind is, I believe, very great.

One final word by way of introduction: I do not approach this examination of the relation of the churches
to the crisis of these times in any carping spirit. Such
problems as today confront us are of such a baffling and
appalling nature that there is, everywhere and every day,
need for the spirit of patience, of humility, and of mutual concern. If the churches are found failing to help
tormented men to grasp and solve their most pressing
problems, it is at least permissible to suggest that other
agencies—schools, press, laboratories, governments—are
not doing much better, if as well.

In asking what part the churches are playing in our
contemporary crisis my greatest concern is for our young
people. It is upon them that the heaviest load of responsibility is falling, and I fear that it is they who see least
hope in their future. We now demand, because of the
pressure of the crisis, that their lives shall be torn up by
the roots. They are taken directly from the classroom to
the army barracks; they are in such a world of insecurity
and controls (it is one indication of the nightmare nature of their world that as the insecurity increases, the
controls increase; or perhaps it is the other way round,
that as the controls increase, the insecurity increases),
they are in such a world of insecurity and controls, I say,
that they cannot try to form families, or to beget and rear
children, or to build up professional or business careers,
or to train for any of the skilled trades without fearing
that at any moment the whole structure of their lives

may be torn apart. Are they finding, *will* they find in Christianity, as exemplified by the churches they know, help in coming to terms with such a demonic world and in restoring it to sanity and order? I am convinced, as I shall say again before this book is ended, that for these young people the paramount issue is not whether what the churches are saying is *true* but whether what they are saying and doing is *relevant* to the situation in which to-day's youth find themselves. If these young people do not believe that the ministry of the churches is relevant to their condition and their problems, how can they be expected to maintain more than casual relations with them?

Against this background, therefore, let us turn to consideration of the manner in which the Christian churches are meeting the ordeal of these times. I wish to direct attention in my first two chapters to the part being played by the Roman Catholic Church. In the third chapter we shall consider the Eastern Orthodox Churches. The fourth chapter will take up World Protestantism, especially in its ecumenical aspects. And in the final chapter we shall look at the American churches, whose problems can be better understood by American Protestant readers after they have considered the problems facing Catholicism, Orthodoxy, and Protestantism elsewhere.

Chapter One

Roman Catholicism in the World Crisis

THE ROMAN CATHOLIC CHURCH today furnishes material for a fascinating study of a mammoth ecclesiastical organization which is on both the defensive and the offensive. Its own leadership tends to stress its defensive position, as I discovered a few years ago during a week spent in daily contact with the Vatican. Protestants tend to be impressed by evidences of its offensive strength. Both aspects must be taken into account if its relation to our contemporary crisis is to be correctly assessed.

Pope Pius XII, an International Diplomat

One indication of the anxiety with which Roman Catholic leadership contemplates the church's position is reflected in the person of the present pope. Pius XII is a trained diplomat. His whole career, before his elevation to the papal throne, had been spent in dealing with governments. His eminence in the church had been won by negotiating agreements with governments, notably with Poland and Hitler Germany. He is the first man in the long history of the papacy to come to that post from the Vatican's secretariat of state. Since his enthronement he has acted as his own secretary of state—likewise a policy without precedent and one which may prove costly to the church in the future, for the pope seems fated to leave the Roman Church, as President Roosevelt, who was also in actuality his own secretary of state, left the United States, without anyone trained to carry on his diplomatic policies after his death.

Pope Pius XII is a man of great austerity of character and intellectual vigor, a member of the aristocratic papal nobility of Rome (as was the great Leo XIII), who consciously prepared for his election by traveling widely through the Western world. He is the only pope who has seen at first hand Great Britain, the United States, and parts of South America. The flexibility, daring, and political nature of his thinking was shown early in his pontificate when he chose the largest number of cardinals ever elevated at one time, and so scattered his choices as to provide his church with at least one native-born cardinal on every continent, including Africa and Australia. In the field of international diplomacy I believe that he has no present equal.

In the last few years, as the pope has felt the end of his reign approaching, he has given increasing attention to matters of church dogma and discipline. Along with this has gone an attempt to depict him to the world as a man of shy friendliness and simple piety, with a strong sense of pastoral concern for all humanity—a conception which found distinguished expression in the personality sketch of the pope by Emmet Hughes in a recent Chris-

tianity issue of *Life*. I do not question the accuracy of
this portrait. But the most valuable service Pius XII has
rendered his church, the thing for which the church was
looking when it elected him and which he has provided
in abundant measure, has been the diplomatic astute-
ness with which he has directed its relations with governments, politics, and social movements during these
years of world upheaval.

Roman Catholicism on the Defensive

The Roman Catholic Church today is on the defensive. Some American Protestants may be surprised by
that assertion, for it is not apparent in this country. But
in Europe, in Latin America, and in many of its largest
Asian mission fields it finds itself under constant attack.
In the brief period since the First World War it has
seen such Catholic strongholds as Poland, Bohemia,
Austria, Hungary, and Croatia break the legal ties which
bound them to the papacy. France disestablished the
church even before the outbreak of that war. Northern
Italy has become a Communist stronghold. Primates of
the church have been sent to prison in Hungary, Poland,
Yugoslavia, and Czechoslovakia. Even the Catholic dictatorships in Spain and Portugal represent a regretted
choice for the papacy; the Church of Rome would much
prefer a "legitimate" Bourbon enthroned in both countries to the present fascist dictatorships. Most Americans appear to have missed the fact that the recent rapprochement between Spain and the United States came
at the very time more and more open criticism of Franco
was being indulged in by members of the Spanish hierarchy. In addition, that hierarchy regards with uncon-
cealed suspicion and distaste Franco's Falange party—

under the dictatorship the only legal party in Spain—and the Falange returns that animosity with interest.

For all these and other reasons, as Pius XII looks out from his palace by the Tiber he must frequently feel like the commander of a besieged fortress, with the besiegers steadily drawing closer to the citadel. He can almost see the red flags flying across the Adriatic, or in such ancient Catholic capitals as Warsaw and Budapest; he can almost hear the shouts of the Red demonstrators in Bologna and Milan. Added to this, he is well aware of the unsatisfactory position of the church in Latin countries. The nominal nature of the adherence of great masses, especially males, in the Latin countries makes increasingly necessary ceaseless manipulation with governments to insure church power and privileges. But this involves political intrigues which too often bring unfavorable popular reactions. Such intrigues likewise frequently tend to involve the fortunes of the church with the fortunes of discreditable political regimes which are doomed to eventual collapse.

The world has recently seen a striking illustration of this in Argentina. Because the final collapse of the malodorous Peron regime was precipitated so largely by the fight in which Peron became involved with the church, it is sometimes forgotten that Peron, in his rise to dictatorial power, was largely the creature of the church. It was church support, bought by his promises to restore to the church special privileges that had been taken away by Argentina's liberal educational legislation of 1884, and other subsequent liberal legislation, which carried Peron to power. Until, for reasons still far from clear, Peron chose to challenge the church by threatening its disestablishment and the withdrawal of the educational controls he had himself given it, the Roman hierarchy was the most conspicuous support of Peron's dictatorship. Here and there a few courageous priests dared to speak out against the outrageous graft and highhanded tyranny of the Peron government, and to warn their church of the perilous position into which it had strayed as the ally of such a disreputable regime. But the Argentine hierarchy was content to play along with Peron until Peron turned on it. Then, with the help of the conservative great landowners and the conservative elements in the armed forces, it quickly struck him down. But the Roman church in Argentina is by no means in the clear today because it is no longer tied up with a scoundrel like Peron. The same old social injustices which made the Argentine masses hail Peron as their champion are still there, and if the church now appears to be in league with the very wealthy owners of great estates and the reactionaries in the military and legal professions who view with such indifference the poverty of the majority of Argentina's people, the pope is enough of a student of history to know that a day of reckoning for the church will certainly come.

Collaboration between the church and such political figures as Franco and Peron is usually rationalized on the ground that dictators of this stripe are a defense against the spread of communism. In the eyes of the papacy, communism is the great enemy. Since it is militant communism which has dispossessed the church from its privileged position in so many countries, and threatens it elsewhere, the Vatican constantly preaches the moral duty of governments to oppose with every measure required the further extension of Communist power. The pope has frequently insisted on his loving, paternal concern for the spiritual welfare of the Russian people and of all people living under Communist rule.

But communism as a political and social system is, in the mind of the Roman church, quite simply, "the enemy." In encyclicals Pius XII has referred to it as "the infernal enemy"—meaning that he regards it as literally the product and agent of the Devil.

Aside from calling on the nations to oppose this enemy, how does the Roman church conduct its defensive against communism? It has adopted many forms of defensive strategy, not excepting the familiar military maxim that "the best defense is an offense." Where its bishops and priests have suffered bodily harm or imprisonment, it has declared excommunicate all participating in such actions. The pope has also decreed the excommunication of all members of Communist parties or persons voting Communist tickets. But these moves are more calculated to gain the notice of the press than to have much actual effect. Active members of Communist parties can be assumed to be, by virtue of that fact, already out of communion with the church. As for the 8 to 10 million who vote Communist in Italy (out of a total of about 17 million voters in a country where 99.6 per cent of the population is listed by the census as Catholic) the number of those defying the Vatican's warning is so huge that the excommunicatory decree of the pope was quickly followed by "interpretations" in the Vatican press which reduced the number actually threatened with such ecclesiastical punishment to the hard core of Communist party leadership—which is of course indifferent to any threats of being excluded from the sacraments.

To a degree which is frequently not appreciated in this country, in countries which have gone Communist the Roman Catholic Church, after a period of stubborn opposition, has given ground. Conspicuous illustrations are Poland and Hungary. In the former, the late Cardinal Hlond favored a policy of accommodation almost from the start. As a result, Catholic bishops and priests took the oath to the Communist government and have been working, under the severe handicap of communism's ingrained and justified suspicion of what the Vatican is up to, to convince the Polish government that they can safely be permitted to carry on their churchly functions, hold much of their former property, and continue to train a new generation of priests without engaging in subversive activities. At one point in 1951 the Polish Communist government actually conferred high decorations on a number of Catholic priests at a public ceremony in Warsaw!

These Communist-decorated priests, however, were members of the so-called "Progressive Catholic" group which *Osservatore Romano*, the Vatican daily newspaper, last August called "near heresy" because it is allegedly veering toward a declaration of independence from the authority of the papacy. There has been in this country for many years a Polish National Catholic Church with a membership of about 300,000. Before World War II it had about the same membership in Poland itself. This church is a member of the World Council of Churches although not yet of the National Council of Churches. The Polish Communists are too realistic to believe that any great proportion of the Polish population can be weaned away from Catholicism— although Poland is said to be heavily sown these days with typical Communist atheistic tracts—but they apparently hope to develop a nationalistic Catholicism with no ties to the Vatican on the order of the Polish

National Catholic Church. It is against this possibility that the Roman hierarchy is fighting today in Poland. Nine bishops and Cardinal Wyszynski are under some form of arrest. Ann Sue Cardwell, whose husband was secretary of the YMCA in Poland for years before Hitler's invasion, wrote an article for *The Christian Century* of February 22, 1955. She pointed out that although the worship services and the catechetical instruction classes of the church continue without interference, the tug-of-war between the priests and laity who are loyal to Rome and the "Progressive Catholics" grows more severe all the time, with some surface indications that the "Progressives" are gaining ground.*

In Hungary, the much rougher treatment given the church, including the brainwashing and imprisonment in 1949 of Cardinal Mindszenty, has likewise brought a measure of accommodation. It is hard to be sure just how far the church has gone in meeting the demands of the Hungarian Communist government, for reports that come through Vatican channels naturally tend to minimize any concessions made by churchmen while reports from government sources in Budapest exaggerate them. But it is known that the entire Hungarian hierarchy has taken the oath of allegiance to the Communist state, and at present is apparently working in such conformity with government regulations that Cardinal

* Events in Poland since the dramatic return to power of Wladislav Gomulka and the release of Cardinal Wyszynski and the Roman Catholic bishops tend to confirm Dr. Hutchinson's analysis. The speed with which Cardinal Wyszynski and the Roman hierarchy came to terms with the Gomulka regime, and the vigor with which they supported Gomulka in the January, 1957 election indicate fear of something worse than Communist persecution—the specter of a national Polish Catholic church, which acknowledges no ties to the Vatican, growing steadily under Russian puppet regime encouragement.

Mindszenty has been reported released from prison, to be secluded in a monastery.†

Much the same thing has happened in Czechoslovakia, although there the bishops tried to water down in the eyes of the public the sensational nature of their decision to bow to the state by instructing priests to make a mental reservation, when taking their oath of allegiance, to the effect that they would obey the laws of the state in so far as these were not in conflict with the laws of God. The Czechoslovakian government has never recognized the existence or legitimacy of this mental reservation, and the hierarchy has done nothing to raise the issue.

In Croatia, the Roman Catholic portion of Yugoslavia, the Catholic clergy have sufficiently bowed to the authority of Marshal Tito's Communist government so that it has been thought safe to release Cardinal Stepinac from prison, though he is confined to his native village and discharges no administrative functions. In Croatia, again, the Vatican's defensive strategy has largely been concentrated on keeping priests from joining the organization of so-called "Patriotic Priests" sponsored by the government—here again, as in Poland, Hungary, and Czechoslovakia, because the *first interest of the pope is to see that no "national" Catholic church, rejecting the authority of the papacy, develops under Communist encouragement. The Vatican always assails the threat of communism in terms of its promotion of atheism, but what it fears far more is the fostering of national forms of Catholicism which have*

† Editor's Note: Associated Press dispatches of October 31, 1956 announced that Cardinal Mindszenty had just been freed from prison by revolutionary forces.

thrown off their allegiance to Rome. The papacy never forgets what happened in England under Henry VIII.

The Growth of Catholic Political Parties in Europe

These have been illustrations of the defensive rearguard actions which the Roman Catholic Church has been compelled to resort to in those parts of postwar Europe where communism has taken over political power. Another, and in some respects more important, tactic which the church is employing in countries that have not gone Communist is the encouragement of church political parties. This is the sort of defense in which an offensive makes the best defense. In western Europe the development of Catholic parties has, since the war, become one of the principal activities of the papally encouraged lay movement known as Catholic Action.

Church parties are an old story in European politics. Holland, for example, has traditionally been ruled by either of two Protestant parties, both so conservative that young Hollanders with the slightest touch of social liberalism have virtually been forced to vote Socialist. Since the war, however, the Catholic party in Holland, with a fairly liberal social program, has gained so much strength that for a number of years the Netherlands has presented the paradoxical spectacle of a Protestant throne by law established taking its policy from a Roman Catholic prime minister.

The growth of Catholic political parties in postwar Europe has been one of the most remarkable phenomena in this confused and desperate period. There are such parties in Italy, France, West Germany (for one must regard the Christian Democratic Union of Chancellor Adenauer as predominantly Catholic), Belgium, and Holland—to say nothing about Portugal and Spain —and in every one they have controlled the government, or at least held the premiership, during most of the postwar years. But the political defensive which the church tries to fight through the medium of these parties, while initially effective, does not work out well in the long run. Why not? Let us look at the situation in Italy and see whether it yields a clue.

The end of the war found the Roman Catholic Church in a very exposed and dangerous position in Italy. Before the war it had had some difficulties in getting along with Mussolini, whom Benedict XV blasted on one occasion in some of the most intemperate language to come from the modern papacy. It had also had a strained relationship with the House of Savoy, the beneficiary of Garibaldi's and Mazzini's destruction of the Papal States. But it had worked out the Lateran treaty with Mussolini and, after that, was on good terms with the monarchy. When both these discredited orders fell—the fascist dictatorship and the weak monarchy—the church knew that it must work fast and hard to keep from sharing in their discrediting.

Fortunately, from the church's point of view, Communist bungling helped—and at almost every turn in Italy's postwar road, when the nation seemed on the point of diving off the deep end into communism, Red blunders have intervened to change the mind of the electorate. The Western allies, then occupying Italy, showed that they were ready to give strong financial and other support to a middle-of-the-road party which could provide peace and order. As a result, Italy passed into the hands of the Christian Democratic party, a Catholic party, with an Austrian who was a former librarian at the Vatican, Alcide de Gasperi, as premier.

The U. S. government has gone to extraordinary lengths to keep first de Gasperi and then his party successors in office. Perhaps in the long run this is turning out to be one of the party's handicaps, for American prestige is no longer very high in Italy—most Italians share the widespread European fear that the United States intends at some future date to try to wipe out the Soviet Union in a nuclear war, and the European peoples have no enthusiasm for the prospect of having that kind of war fought over them and their homes—and the Christian Democratic party, tagged as the American-favored party, has suffered accordingly.

On the surface it would appear that at no time since the Papal States were taken away from Pius IX has the Vatican held as much political power in Italy as it exerts today. Nevertheless, there are astute men in the Vatican who know that the masses of Italy—especially the peasant masses—are suffering from grievous social injustices which, unless righted, will certainly and in the not too distant future produce an explosion. The Vatican therefore encouraged de Gasperi and the Christian Democrats to announce a program of land reform and tax reform. It is on a program of this sort that the Catholic party has carried Italian elections since the war. Yet very little has been done to carry its promised reforms into effect, with the consequence that once again the Christian Democrats seem on the verge of losing control of Parliament (with many of their members shifting toward the Nenni wing of the Socialist party, which favors collaboration with the Communists) and the Communists are widely believed to be closer to taking over the government than they have ever been. The policy of sweet reasonableness now being followed by the Kremlin will help along this increase of Communist strength.

Why is the Christian Democratic party in Italy thus petering out? First, because though it was comparatively easy to combine bourgeois, aristocratic, and clerical elements to oppose the Reds, once the elections have been won, the disparate interests of those elements have prevented the cabinet and parliamentary majority from agreeing on any affirmative policy. Second, because most of the land which must be redistributed if the peasants are to be satisfied is owned either by the church or by the papal nobility which lives in luxury in Rome, and neither the church nor the nobility will give it up. And if tax burdens are to be redistributed to placate the industrial workers who now carry almost all the Italian tax load, they will have to be shifted to the church, the papal nobility, and the factory owners who are high in the councils of the church party—and none of the three will permit that to happen. So, little by little, Italy's common people have lost confidence in the ability of the church party to make any decided difference in their hard lot, and the vigor of the party has seeped away. It is headed for history's ashcan.‡

I have told this story of Italy at some length because it shows, in essentials, what finally undermines all the Catholic church parties. The conservative elements which dominate them cannot agree on constructive social programs sufficient to satisfy the social demands of the masses. That is what has happened in France where

‡ Since this was written, Russia's cruelty and repression of freedom in Hungary, and her return to overt Stalinist ruthlessness have driven millions of disillusioned members from the Communist party in Italy. The consequent probability of increased support for the Christian Democratic party in no way ameliorates its fundamental weaknesses, and probably only delays the ultimate fate predicted for it by Dr. Hutchinson.

the MRP, the Catholic party, which took over with such promise after the war, has floundered until in the recent elections it lost so much ground in the National Assembly that it now seems fated to fade out almost as rapidly and completely as the party of General de Gaulle. And now, though a little more slowly, the same thing is happening in West Germany, where the CDU which put Chancellor Adenauer in office has been in the main a coalition of conservative Rhineland and Bavarian Catholics with the industrialists of the Ruhr. The combination has supported a foreign policy which the Western allies like—since it consists mainly of rearmament and membership in the Western alliance—but it has had no domestic policy with appeal to the West German voters. The CDU now seems unlikely either to last as long or to play as important a political role henceforth as did the old Catholic Center party in the years of the Hohenzollerns and the Weimar Republic.

On the Defensive in Far-Eastern Mission Fields

From this hasty sketch it will be clear, I trust, that in its political relationships in postwar Europe the Roman church has been almost everywhere on the defensive, and that its varied strategies of defense are not yielding very impressive long-run results. I must not leave this phase of our subject, however, without briefly pointing out that the papal church has also been thrown on the defensive in its greatest mission fields in Asia, and that the defensive measures taken there have also been less than successful.

East and southeast Asia, ever since the days of St. Francis Xavier, has been Catholicism's most coveted mission field. Catholic missions preceded Protestant by more than two centuries, and have been marked by heroic service, often leading to martyrdom. In point of scholarship, likewise, the Catholic missionaries have surpassed their Protestant rivals. As one who witnessed Catholic missions in operation in China for a number of years before the upheaval which began in 1926, I am glad to pay my tribute to the devotion and the saintly character of many of the missionary priests I encountered. It is my judgment that on the whole Roman Catholic missions at that time were better administered and more effective than were the Protestant.

But the storm which has swept over the Far East in the wake of the Second World War and the rise of communism as a Far Eastern power has not spared Roman Catholicism. In some places, it has hit the papal church even harder than the Protestant churches. And this has happened despite the fact that the pope, early discerning the force of Asian nationalistic movements, moved much more rapidly and intelligently than most Protestant mission bodies to realign Catholic missions to prepare to meet the storm. In both China and India, the Roman Catholic Church had been provided with an almost completely national episcopacy by the end of the war. The cardinal and archbishops in China were all Chinese by 1946; the same is now true in India. Where nationals of other countries continue as bishops, this is only in recently formed and still undeveloped dioceses; it is understood to be an interim arrangement that will be ended at the first moment a national clergy capable of taking over administrative responsibilities has been developed. But the nationalization of episcopacy and clergy has not proved a defensive measure sufficient to protect Catholicism in the Far

East from the fury of the nationalistic, communistic anti-Western storm.

In the countries where the Roman church has suffered most severely two defensive strategies were tried. In China, under the leadership of the brilliant and daring Archbishop Paul Yu-ping, the church threw itself into the political arena, going all-out in support of Chiang Kai-shek and his Kuomintang party, with the archbishop himself becoming a member of the praesidium of the Legislative Yuan, or parliament. To be sure, many Protestant clergy and missionaries gave public and unremitting support to the Kuomintang, while the U. S. government, in its efforts to bolster up the shaky regime of Chiang Kai-shek went to the unusual length of making a Protestant missionary the American ambassador to China. But Archbishop Yu-ping made the Catholic opposition to the Communists and support of Chiang Kai-shek much more unequivocal and much more politically active than the Protestants ever did—as Chiang Kai-shek himself complained to me in Nanking in 1946. The inevitable consequence was that when the Communists won, and Chiang Kai-shek and the remnants of the Kuomintang were forced to flee to Formosa, the Catholic hierarchy felt the full weight of Communist wrath, and the church ever since has lived most precariously. To its honor be it said, however, that there has been little response to efforts to form a Chinese "national" Catholic church; that there has been almost none of that repudiation of its relations with Rome or of the ministry of missionaries which has been so general throughout Chinese Protestantism; and that both missionaries, Chinese clergy, and laity have proved their readiness to endure torture even to the extreme of martyrdom in a fashion which, I am sure, will one day bear fruit in the revival of Chinese Catholicism.

In Indo-China, where the church had lived complacently under the patronage of the decadent French colonial regime, its first effort to defend itself against the rising tide of nationalism and communism, took the form of looking to the French for protection. Two native Catholic bishops in North Vietnam sought to hold the dikes by transforming their dioceses into virtually independent sovereignties, with their own armies—a sort of Oriental throwback to the old days when bishops and archbishops rode at the head of their feudal forces in medieval Europe. But none of these things sufficed, as we know. The Communists overran the north; the militant bishops were forced to flee; and the future of the church in what has been the most Catholic portion of the East Asia mainland now seems largely to depend on the future of the American-supported government which an ardent Catholic layman, Ngo Dinh Diem, is struggling hard to develop to sufficient strength in South Vietnam to resist the pressure of the Communist north.

India presents still another problem to the papal church. The Catholic community there has been an important one, especially around the French and Portuguese possessions and in the south, where a large portion of the so-called Jacobite church acknowledges the authority of the pope. The pope has gone even further in India than in China to nationalize the church, but the connection between Catholic interests and the refusal of Portugal to follow the French example in returning to the Republic of India its minute colonies on the west coast (the largest, Goa, where the bones of St. Francis Xavier are preserved, is smaller than a Louisiana parish) is making the church a target for attack by extreme Indian nationalists. Although the pope assured Mr. Nehru that the Vatican had no misgivings as to what would happen to Catholic shrines or the Catholic population of Goa if India took over that colony, Portuguese ecclesiastics there and in Portugal have not been so conciliatory, and the Roman Catholic Church throughout India is having a hard time as a consequence. Catholic bishops have been prominent in recent protests to Prime Minister Nehru against antimissionary measures taken by the authorities in two or three states of the Republic.

As one surveys the Far East today, it becomes plain that the only country in which Catholicism is not on the defensive, but rather is pursuing an actively aggressive course, is in the Philippines.

So we face the paradox that in its political relationships the Roman Catholic Church today is on the defensive almost everywhere except where Protestant traditions of toleration and Protestant social resistance to the Communist lure free it for an aggressive presentation of its own cause. But in aspects other than political the Roman Catholic Church is on the offensive.

Chapter Two

The Roman Catholic Offensive

In the preceding chapter an attempt was made to sketch the varied nature of the defensive strategy which the Roman Catholic Church, under the guidance of Pope Pius XII, is following to defend its interests in Europe, Latin America, and Asia. It is, I suggested, a strategy largely based on the conviction that communism is *the* enemy which the church has to face, that the purpose of communism which the church most fears is not so much the spread of atheism among the masses in Communist countries—although this is a long-range end of education in Communist schools—as fostering the establishment of national Catholic churches which will cut their ties with the papacy. Then it was suggested that although this may prove an effective strategy for the immediate present, it is of dubious worth for the decades ahead since it almost always involves the papal church forces in alliances with ultra-conservative and even reactionary groups.

31

In this chapter we shall turn the picture over and look at it from the other side. The Roman church is not only on the defensive; it is likewise in many parts of the world and in many ways conducting a great offensive to win men to acceptance of the Bishop of Rome as head of the one true, holy, apostolic Christian church and the vice-regent of Jesus Christ on earth. This offensive is being pressed with a vigor and devotion never surpassed in the long history of the Roman communion. We feel its impact throughout this country; it is also making itself felt in other traditionally Protestant countries, such as England, Scotland, and Holland. Let us look at some of its varied manifestations.

On the Offensive, Socially and Industrially

First of all, let me draw your attention to the offensive social and industrial battle which Roman Catholicism is waging. There is nothing more evident in contemporary Europe than the defection of the laboring masses from the churches. This is as true in Protestant as in Catholic countries. If I were presenting the difficulties of the position in which postwar European Protestantism finds itself, I should be forced to give much attention to this drift toward indifference on the part of the working classes. But the popes realized this was happening before Protestant leadership sensed it, or at least became exercised about it, and they have led their church in a mighty effort to reclaim the workers ever since Leo XIII in 1891 issued his historic encyclical, *Rerum Novarum*.

Those who are familiar with the social encyclicals and pronouncements of recent popes know how sensational, to Europe's possessing classes, have been some of the positions taken by the papacy ever since Leo XIII, sixty-five years ago, agreed with Karl Marx that property and wealth have their origin in the labor of men and that, in the words of *Rerum Novarum*, "it may be truly said that it is only by the labor of working men that states grow rich."

By the time Pius XI, on the fortieth anniversary in 1931 of the issuance of *Rerum Novarum*, followed it with his more sweeping encyclical *Quadragesimo Anno*, that pope was ready to declare openly what had caused the papacy to enter this social struggle. It was, said that great pope, "those thousands of Catholic workers who have left the church . . . largely because the whole system of industry and business long ago repudiated the law of Christ concerning such matters. And the captains of industry have gone their way regardless of Christ's law because their greed was too much for the restrictions which that law would lay on them." In other words, the present system of industry in the Western world, capitalism, is a repudiation of Christianity, and the church must go out to change it as part of its apostolic, evangelistic mission.

Now here is something for contemporary Protestantism to think about. If one great branch of the church, speaking through its allegedly infallible head, is ready thus to denounce the social order in which we all live, can the other branches be indifferent on the subject or silent? You are aware, I am sure, of the outcry which is frequently raised by Protestants with conservative social viewpoints over what they claim is unwarranted attention to social and industrial questions—the churches poking their noses into matters which are none of their business. Both the National Council of Churches and the World Council of Churches have been under heavy fire for this. The latest attack, launched by Mr. J. Howard Pew of the big oil interests, and picked up and broadcast by David Lawrence and Raymond Moley in *U.S. News & World Report* and *Newsweek*, makes precisely this charge the basis for advice to Christian laymen to withdraw their support from the National Council of Churches. On the other hand, Carl McIntire and his ultrafundamentalist American and International Councils of Churches by implication promise these well-heeled laymen that if they will switch their financial support to the McIntire organizations, those can be relied on to confine their attention to the sort of "preaching the gospel" which ignores all social issues.

The popes, since Leo XIII began the great shift of the papal church from the social reactionism to which Pius IX tried to commit it, have been more outspoken than such bodies as the National and World Council of Churches have ever been on social issues. In their hope of winning back "those thousands of Catholic workers who have left the church," they have not hesitated to declare modern capitalism as sinful as communism. Listen to the present pope in an exhortation which he addressed to the Roman priesthood in September, 1950. After speaking of the priest's duty to combat communism, Pius XII proceeded: "Other priests demonstrate, similarly, cowardice and uncertainty when confronted by the economic system which is known as capitalism, the grave consequences of which the church has never failed to denounce. . . . The errors of the two economic systems [communism and capitalism] and the dangerous consequences which derive from them, must convince all, and especially the priests, to remain faithful to the social doctrine of the church and to spread its knowledge and personal application." This is not some unrepresentative Catholic radical lumping capitalism and communism together and exhorting the Roman priesthood to get rid of all cowardice and uncertainty in condemning both; this is *the pope*, the head of the church, the occupant of the throne of Peter, the man who claims, as Christ's vice-regent, to speak before all others as God's representative on earth.

The "social doctrine of the church," of which the present pope spoke in the passage just quoted, is a sort of medieval guild socialism, a true corporative state— not the simulation of such a state which Mussolini claimed his fascism was trying to set up in Italy. It is based on the Thomistic conception of the nature of property, with justice in the distribution of the fruits of labor insured by church control of the economic order. It does not deny property rights as such, but it requires that property shall be subordinate to human rights and that the product of society shall be so equitably distributed that all shall have a stake in the maintenance of the social order, with none deprived of its benefits or feeling themselves relegated to what the sociologists call an "out-group." The best official outline of this papally approved social order is to be found in the encyclical of Pius XI, *Quadragesimo Anno*. We cannot go into a detailed analysis of this papal sketch of what a Christian society would be like, but the thing to note is this: it can be presented to the laboring masses in the present crisis of capitalism with as revolutionary an aspect as communism. It is a social offensive by the Roman Catholic Church with great insight into the failings of our present Western society and with even greater boldness in proposing *fundamental* changes in that society.

Nor must it be thought that the papal attack on social injustice has had effect only in the churches of Europe. The social encyclicals are in fact the basis on which the National Catholic Welfare Conference came into being in this country and is developing into a virtual General Headquarters for American Catholicism. It was Msgr. John A. Ryan, the principal American champion of the papal social encyclicals, who led in the formation of what is now the National Catholic Welfare Conference, during the First World War, and as long as Dr. Ryan lived he made its social action department the most active part of this central Catholic organization. To be sure, today the NCWC has become such a vast and powerful body, with its architecturally striking headquarters building cheek-by-jowl with the largest embassies in Washington, that the American hierarchy has moved in and taken over most of its direction. But there is no diminution in the social emphasis which the NCWC gives to American Catholic teaching. At the present moment, on the most controversial social question affecting the American future, the Roman Catholic Church is taking its position against racial discrimination with a forthrightness and courage that puts to shame a large part of Protestantism.

When the Roman Catholic Church first made clear its intention to end racial segregation in its communion in the South, I heard a good deal of cynical comment among Protestants, as doubtless many of us did. "Oh, sure," these cynics said, "a Catholic bishop in rural North Carolina can crack down on a church which refuses to let whites and Negroes take the sacraments together. But how many Catholics, and particularly Negro Catholics, are there in North Carolina? In a minority situation of that kind, you get no real test of a church's position." But now the issue has been put to the test in the great archdioceses of New Orleans and

St. Louis, and in both the archbishops have stood up to it with magnificent courage and with astute intelligence regarding the relation of their local situation to the long-range, world-wide future of their church. The Roman Catholic bishops and archbishops who are hewing to the line on this social issue, often in the face of the most intense opposition from many of their laity, know that they have behind them the support of the American hierachy and the National Catholic Welfare Conference, while the American bishops and the NCWC rest back for *their* support on the impregnable backing of the papal social encyclicals from Leo XIII down to the present Pius XII.

Of course this social offensive of the papal church does not always have smooth sailing. The difficulties it can get into have recently been given spectacular illustration by the struggle over the so-called worker-priests in France. In modern times the Vatican has had one tussle after another with the church in France, which seems to have retained a spirit of independence from tight control by the ultramontanists in Rome which keeps the papal bureaucracy uneasy as to what is transpiring in this country beyond the Alps where the spirit of the French Revolution is by no means dead. We cannot pause to summarize these past difficulties. But the story of what happened to the worker-priests is so recent, and has such melancholy warnings for the future, that it needs to be looked at.

The worker-priests, as they came to be known, were a part of the Mission de France, to give it its official name, which was launched under the patronage of the Archbishop of Paris, the saintly late Cardinal Suhard, shortly after the war. The original impulse for its launching was the publication of a book by two Dominicans who, after careful investigation, found that not more than 4 million of the 40 million Frenchmen retained any vital ties with the church. France, said the book, was as pagan a mission field as any on earth. The Mission de France, which resulted, was made up of Dominicans, Jesuits, and diocesan priests who set out to live with the people and share fully in their experiences and problems, in an effort to win back their confidence and, eventually, to bring them back into the church. Half the members of the mission went into the rural villages, and the other half—about a hundred priests—into industry. It was this latter group, the worker-priests, which eventually fell afoul of the Vatican and was ordered broken up.

There is not space to quote at length the communications which have passed back and forth between the condemned priests and their ecclesiastical superiors. Some of the letters refusing to obey the commands of the French hierarchy—which itself stood out against pressure from Rome for a long time—are as noble expressions of prophetic dedication as any modern church has produced. But the essence of what happened was this: These hundred priests left their monasteries and rectories, doffed their clerical garb and went into the dock section of Marseilles, the Renault auto works of Paris, and scores of other industrial centers. They took jobs, they joined the unions, many of them rose to leadership in labor unions. They were, in a word, grappling with communism for the souls of the French workers right where the workers lived and felt privation and muttered at social injustice. But this complete exposure to the Communist "enemy," unfortunately for the worker-priests, had an effect on some of them that their bishops had not foreseen. They became, in some instances, convinced that the Communist analysis of the weaknesses and evils of the French industrial order was correct. A very few became avowed Communists. One or two were incautious enough to write books or articles which virtually endorsed communism, not only as a correct analysis of what was wrong with France, but as the only social and political movement sufficiently thoroughgoing and courageous to do anything effective to remedy the situation.

The consequence was papal condemnation. Orders came from Rome, finally passed along by the French hierarchy, that these priests were to withdraw from the labor unions, give up manual labor, return to priestly retreats for re-education, renew the wearing of clerical garb and of course repudiate all sympathy for Communist activities. Later, these orders were somewhat modified to permit a limited number of hours a day for mingling with the industrial workers, but on a basis which made impractical any actual participation in factory labor. And the ban against union activity stood. About thirty-five of the worker-priests, including, I believe, all the members of the monastic orders, bowed to episcopal authority, but up to the present the great majority of the diocesan priests have refused to do so. The open letter in which they announced their refusal has been published throughout the French press and made a deep impression on the French public. So much so, in fact, that the French bishops are moving with extreme caution against the recalcitrants. But the whole episode has done the prestige of the papal church, with regard to its declared interest in improving the lot of the workers, no good in France. And on the other hand, it has shocked the Vatican to discover the possibility that priests who come into such intimate contact with the life and problems of the working classes may prove susceptible to the appeal of extreme doctrines of social revolution—even in some instances to the lure of communism. It is safe to predict that the Vatican will hesitate a long time before approving the formation in any other country of apostolates to industrial workers patterned after the worker-priests of France.

The temptation is almost irresistible to pursue further consideration of this social offensive in which Roman Catholicism is today seeking to win back the active allegiance of Europe's working masses. But we must turn now to another aspect of the contemporary Catholic offensive—one of equal boldness, though in an entirely different field and pursued by quite different means. This is its offensive in the intellectual world.

On the Offensive Intellectually

I do not need to tell my readers of the intellectual shock which all Christian thinking has suffered since the rise of seventeenth and eighteenth century rationalism, with its skepticism or outright rejection of old ideas of revelation and its assertion that human reason is the most reliable agency by which man can gain access to Truth. This undermining of the old conceptions reached its climax in the middle of the last century with the emergence of the modern physical sciences. There are still those, in the churches and outside the churches, who think that Charles Darwin gave Christianity its deathblow, if his teaching on natural selection in the origin and development of species is not completely and finally repudiated. Toward the end of the nineteenth century President Andrew D. White of Cornell University wrote his book, *The Warfare of Science and Religion,* and I note that it has recently been re-issued. It deserves such re-issuance, though the conflict is no longer of the sort Dr. White was writing about. It is sufficient to say that, with the application of modern methods of historical investigation to the Bible, in all the Christian world outside the Roman Catholic Church and the fundamentalist churches and sects the whole conception of revelation has changed.

But the intellectual problem which educated Protestantism faced in the closing decades of the last century was as nothing compared with that faced by the papal church. Its difficulties were intensified and compounded by the fact that from 1846 to 1878—the longest reign in the history of the papacy—there sat on the throne of St. Peter that tragic figure, Pius IX. Friends who have lived in villages in northern Italy tell me that peasant mothers there still try to frighten their children into obedience by threatening that "Pio Nono" will get them if they don't behave, just as in southern Ireland mothers still warn their disobedient offspring against falling into the hands of Cromwell. I cannot stop to trace the dismal way in which Pius IX—who became pope with such a reputation as a liberal that the U. S. Congress passed a resolution of congratulation and voted to send a minister to the papal court, after he had been shell-shocked by the revolutionary spirit which swept over Europe in 1848 and '49, threatening the survival of the Papal States (and eventually taking them away from him)—swung all the way over to the most extreme reaction. Pius IX placed the Roman church in complete opposition to the whole spirit and content of modern scholarship, both by his proclamation of the dogmas of the Immaculate Conception and Papal Infallibility (the latter especially fought bitterly to the moment of its proclamation by Lord Acton, the great

British historian and the most distinguished scholar modern Catholicism has produced) and even more by the issuance of his *Syllabus of Errors*, that compilation of liberal ideas in theology, church discipline, social relations, education, and all forms of intellectual activity which a good Catholic may not believe and remain a good Catholic. To this day, the *Syllabus* hangs like a millstone around the necks of liberal-minded Catholics, especially in countries like Great Britain and the United States, and efforts to ignore it or to suggest that it no longer represents authoritative Catholic teaching have to reckon with such a plain declaration as this in the *Catholic Encyclopedia*: "The Syllabus . . . is a decision given by the pope speaking as universal teacher and judge to Catholics the world over. All Catholics, therefore, are bound to accept the Syllabus. Exteriorially they may neither in word nor in writing oppose its contents; they must also assent to it interiorly."

What Pius IX was intent on doing was to open a great Catholic offensive against the the whole liberal intellectual trend in the West. These standards of dogma which flout every canon of historical investigation (the Immaculate Conception and Papal Infallibility) and this scholarship operating within given intellectual limits set by the church have given Catholic scholars a norm of authority in an often chaotic intellectual world. At the same time, however, they have set them apart from that unlimited freedom of inquiry which is the first premise of modern scholarly life. What Pius IX began, Leo XIII—certainly the greatest of modern popes and some would argue the greatest of all popes—continued. In his *Aeternis Patris*, issued the year after his elevation, Leo made the medieval scholastic philosophy of St. Thomas Aquinas the standard for the church, and in his *Providentissimus Deus* (1893) he condemned what he called the "disquieting tendencies" in biblical interpretation "which, if they prevailed, could not fail to destroy the inspired and supernatural character of the Bible."

This determination by the papacy to fence off an intellectual world for Catholicism of its own, in which the groping and often confused minds of this age can find a certainty and an authority elsewhere lacking, has been pushed rigorously in each succeeding papal reign. It was the overarching purpose of Pius X, the saintly pontiff who became the first pope to be canonized in 242 years. His condemnation of "modernism" in theology and excommunication of priests infected with that virus, was followed by imposition of the special oath which all professors in Roman Catholic seminaries, colleges and schools, and all ordinands have to take to support "all the condemnations, declarations, and proscriptions" against modern biblical interpretation in the sixty-five propositions condemned by the Inquisition and listed in Pius X's decree of 1907, *Lamentabili.* This intellectual strategy has come clearly into the open again in the reign of the present pope by his action in proclaiming, in 1950, the dogma of the Assumption of the Virgin, by issuing in the same year his encyclical, *Humani Generis,* and by the address which he made to the church's cardinals, archbishops, and bishops in November, 1954.

Even in his bull proclaiming the dogma of the Assumption of the Virgin, Pius XII has no historical or scriptural authority to adduce. The Assumption rests entirely on tradition, and it is a tradition with such a murky and disputed background that one wonders what goes on in the mind of a Catholic trained in methods of historical research and scholarship—such a man, for ex-

ample, as Carlton J. H. Hayes, former ambassador to
Spain and former head of the department of history at
Columbia University—when he is faced with the demand that he believe such an anti-intellectual conception on pain of risking eternal damnation. Perhaps that
is the sort of Catholic Pope Pius had in mind when, in
his address to the bishops, he said: "Even though to
someone certain declarations of the church may not
seem proved by the arguments put forward, his obliga-
tion to obey still remains." Tertullian could say, *Credo
quia incredibile*, but that certainly is not the voice of
this age.

But *Humani Generis*, the encyclical of 1950, is in
many respects the most revealing document on the intellectual policy of the modern papacy. It lays down the
limits inside which Roman Church scholarship must op-
erate. Prof. Georges A. Barrois, once a Dominican on
the faculty of colleges in France and the Catholic University at Washington, D.C., who is now a professor at
Princeton Theological Seminary, has pointed out that
Humani Generis was produced to crack down on the
recent suggestions of certain Catholic scholars—especially
a number of Dominicans and Jesuits in France—looking
toward a redefinition of the church's conception of
dogma, tradition, and theology. To understand how
brusquely all such innovations in thought are condemned and how strictly the control of the pope over
the limits of research and speculation is asserted, one
must read the full text of this too little known document. Unfortunately, it has appeared in English trans-
lation only once, so far as I know, in this country—in
the *New York Times* of Aug. 22, 1950—and Prof. Barrois says that this version for reasons unknown omits
two important paragraphs.

In this encyclical Pius XII professes sympathy with the work of scholars, but insists this must not go beyond what the Vatican says is permissible. When certain French Dominicans proposed that dogma and theology be seen as products of the time in which they emerge and interpreted in this light—divine truth being, indeed, eternal, but man's perception inevitably limited by his finite nature—and when certain French Jesuits proposed that the church go back to the tradition of the very early church fathers (and I do not need to point out what *that* would do to the three recently proclaimed dogmas of Papal Infallibility, the Immaculate Conception, and the Assumption of the Virgin), they were wandering into forbidden territory. One proof that they were so doing, the encyclical holds, is to be seen in their increasing friendliness with theologians of non-Roman churches. This trend toward a common position on important questions of Christian teaching the pope condemns as the work of misguided advocates of what he calls "irenics"—in itself a revealing commentary on the papacy's oft-declared desire for Christian reunion.

In conclusion, this encyclical resorts to a specific illustration to show Catholic scholars what the limits are within which they must confine their work. The first three chapters of Genesis, it says, must be accepted as literally and historically true. The creation and fall happened exactly as reported there. There is no myth; and, if the sacred writer did employ some metaphor, that does not affect the historical accuracy of the whole account. Since the pope says this is truth—historic and scientific as well as theological truth—it becomes for every Catholic scholar what some philosophers call a "given."

The present pope's allocution to his bishops is notable for two things: its flat assertion that the church has authority to settle issues of politics, economics, and social relationships entirely outside the issues Pius XII says men call "matters strictly religious," and, in the second place, its scarcely veiled warning to Catholic laity against wandering outside papally prescribed boundaries either in their thinking or writing.

It must have been noticeable to many Protestant readers that in recent years much of the effective presentation of Catholic thought on issues in dispute with other churches has come from laymen. One thinks immediately of the late Gilbert K. Chesterton, the living Christopher Dawson, the novelist Graham Greene, or the lay editors of *Commonweal* in this country. Such a distinguished Catholic layman as Jacques Maritain, now a professor at Princeton, despite the papal rejection of the principle of separation of church and state, in his book, *The Rights of Man and Natural Law*, proceeds to work out a sketch of church-state relationships which most Protestants would have no great difficulty in adjusting to their own views on such relationships. When one reads a book like this, one wonders whether the Vatican intends to allow Catholic laity a leeway in discussion which is to be forbidden the priesthood. The precedent of Lord Acton, already mentioned, comes to mind. But even Acton had to fall silent after Papal Infallibility had been proclaimed. Is the papacy now moving toward curbing the venturesomeness of lay Catholic writers? The pope's allocution contains a long, carefully worded but unmistakable warning to "moderns," as the pope calls them, who "think that the leadership and vigilance of the church is not to be suffered by one who is grown up." "To be an adult and to have put off the things of childhood," the pope continues, "is one thing, and [it is] quite another to be an adult and not to be subject to the guidance and government of legitimate authority." In other words, lay writers on any and all subjects over which the pope claims authority—and this same allocution has shown this includes just about everything related to human life—are warned to watch their step.

Now this may look more like a defensive than an offensive Vatican strategy. But I think it is the latter—and not only in the sense that an offense is sometimes the most effective defense. This is an offensive in the intellectual realm, as should appear if we study closely the nature of that realm today. Not to go into this at length, let me summarize by saying that the intellectual world today is in ferment verging on chaos. Its old standards are gone—what, for instance, is a modern poem or a novel? A visit to a gallery of modern art or a concert of modern music may be enthralling—to some people, that is—but for most of us it is a venture into the inexplicable. After a roomful of Picassos we give three cheers for Grandma Moses, and after a page of *Finnegans Wake* we scramble frantically in the bookcase to make sure no one has thrown away the precious volumes of Jane Austen. The answers that the intellectual was getting from science and the materialistic world-view a few decades ago no longer satisfy him. He feels the limits of his intelligence; he looks in vain for guideposts in his Wasteland; he is a man, or a woman, at sea. In Plato's phrase, "Whirl is king, having cast out Zeus."

It is to this inhabitant of the whirling intellectual world, whose mind—like the music in the popular song of a few years ago—is going round and round but coming out nowhere, that the Roman Catholic Church can come and say, "Are there questions too great, too difficult, for your finite mind? Of course there are. And they are the ultimate questions—the questions concerning your soul and its eternal destiny. What you need to understand is that all your learning will never answer those questions; that its very pretense of trying to do so is only leading you farther and farther from any certainty of Truth. But here is Mother Church, to whom ultimate Truth has been divinely revealed, equipped and disciplined to mediate that Truth to you through the agency of an infallible papacy and a priesthood endowed with limitless sacramental powers. All that is required of you is that in this realm of ultimates where no rational guide can ever lead you to certainty, you shall by faith accept the assurance of this perfect vessel of Divine Revelation—the one, true, holy, catholic, and apostolic church—and rest back in comfort and assurance of soul." Many a confused and desperate intellectual, as you well know, is responding to that appeal. It is an effective offensive strategy in the case of men and women as different as Evelyn Waugh and Jacques Maritain and Barbara Ward and Heywood Broun and Clare Boothe Luce, largely because it rejects so uncompromisingly the pretensions of the finite mind of man and insists that in the realm of Ultimates only a word of Authority claiming supermundane credentials can have any worth.

There is one other aspect of this intellectual offensive which must be noted, though not at the length it deserves. In a way, this is an anti-intellectual offensive. What we have been considering is the steps taken from Pius IX through Pius XII to set apart Roman Catholic thinking from the characteristic thinking of our day, and thus to offer a harbor of refuge for intellectuals. But there is also an offensive aimed at the minds of those with no intellectual pretensions who nevertheless are

seeking spiritual satisfactions beyond those experienced
in the past. This consists in the tremendous emphasis
now being placed by the church on the cultivation of
the cult of the Virgin, mother of God and Co-Redemptrix of humanity. This sentimentalized form of popular
worship (for that, despite all theological protestations
to the contrary, is what this appeal to the intercession
of Mary is fast becoming) is sweeping the rank-and-file
Roman Catholic population of the world. Any of you
who are conversant with what is happening in Catholic
congregations, not only in consequence of the procla-
mations of new dogmas concerning the Virgin, but in
the multiplication and exploitation of shrines where the
Virgin is supposed to have made recent miraculous ap-
pearances (the Catholic historian, Philip Hughes, lists
four such in France alone during the last century; and
the appearance of Fatima in Portugal—now the most
exploited of all because it has to do directly with the
church's struggle against communism—is so recent that
one of the children to whom the appearance was granted
is still alive); you who have seen the multiplication of
novenas where the intervention of the Virgin is invoked
for every purpose from winning a husband or a job to
curing tuberculosis, or the development of a popular
Catholic hymnology of the "O mother dear, remember
me," variety—any of you who know of these things will
understand at once what I am talking about.

The famous Swiss psychologist, C. G. Jung, explains
this as evidence of this ancient church's wisdom in per-
ceiving that the female sex is achieving the position of
dominance hitherto held by the male, so that by the
deification of the Virgin the Godhead will be transformed into a feminine deity. (It is on the basis of this
interpretation that Jung has called the proclamation of

the Assumption of the Virgin the most important development in religion since the Reformation.) But I see no need for such a psychological tour de force to explain what is happening. Rather, I believe, this is a part of Rome's intellectual offensive which seeks to compensate for the rigid mental discipline it is imposing in this Western world where the watchword is freedom by encouraging its adherents in a form of worship centered on a figure totally divorced from all issues of ethics and empiric truth, but compounded of sentimentalized concepts of love to which tired and bruised souls can turn emotionally and find an anodyne.

Now, far too hastily, I must close with a sort of footnote to all I have been saying about the offensive strategy that is at present characteristic of the Roman church in most of the United States and with an attempted summary of the total world position of that great communion.

On the Offensive Statistically

Cardinal Stritch, whose Chicago archdiocese is the largest in world Catholicism, attracted some newspaper attention recently by a claim that Protestantism is no longer the majority religion in this country. We received numbers of indignant letters in the offices of *The Christian Century*, demanding that we rebuke the cardinal and reassert the fact that this is a Protestant nation. We did not do so, for several reasons. It is, of course, true that so far as statistics go the latest church statistics show that out of a total population of 160 million, 97.5 millions are on church rolls. Of these, 32.5 million are reckoned as Roman Catholics and 5.5 million Jews. This leaves 50 million Protestants. But there are several things to be said about these figures. In the first place, they are church figures, and if there is any form of statistic less reliable than a church statistic, I don't know what it is. How many of you who may be preachers, when you have gone to a new charge, have been able to find all the members your predecessor reported? In the second place, 50 million Protestants do not comprise a majority of the American population—and that was all that Cardinal Stritch had actually said in the interview which so angered some who did not look closely at his words.

But more importantly, our paper did not object to the cardinal's statement because he was simply reflecting an opinion which has become general through the American hierarchy in recent years, and for which there is some basis. The Roman Catholic bishops in this country are now convinced that Protestant membership claims are inflated so far out of all relation to realities that theirs, in terms of numbers of actual communicants, is the larger body. And if this is denied, they hold that Catholicism is certainly the majority church in American cities, which every census shows to be the steadily increasing centers of our national power. It is this simple basic change in Catholicism's conception of its own status which explains the sudden adoption of an offensive posture by the American hierarchy, and why the American people suddenly find themselves confronted with such demands as for the establishment of a U. S. Embassy at the Vatican and for state aid for church schools. (In this connection, may I remark in passing that it astonishes me to discover Protestant leaders in the South who, in proposing to get around the school segregation issue by abolishing public schools and providing state subventions to make possible attendance by white children at segregated church private schools, fail to perceive that if they carry this into effect they will thereby throw away the whole Protestant case against state funds for church schools. The quibble that the money will go to families, and not to the church schools directly, will not save the principle, for it *is* a quibble, and no principle under attack from forces as strong as those of Catholicism in this country can survive on such a shaky foundation.)

Yet it is not only in respect to such political issues as the Vatican embassy and the subvention of parochial schools that there is in this country a Roman Catholic offensive with which to reckon. The papal church is showing more courage and a more long-range perspicacity in its dealing with the race problem and in proving its friendship for the organized labor movement than is a large portion of American Protestantism. It has a much more sustained and professionally competent evangelism aimed at the general public through mass communication media—television, radio, magazines, and the press—than anything Protestantism can show. And any politician, social worker, or reformer can tell you that in almost any large city in the United States, if you want to get anything of importance done, from electing a party ticket to establishing a new method for caring for orphans, one of the first things you need to do is to go around to the Catholic diocesan chancellery and find out whether you can get its support. There are a few large municipalities where things of importance can be brought to pass against the opposition of the Roman diocesan authorities, but not many.

Yet despite the vigor with which Roman Catholicism is pressing toward its goals in this country, and its increasing influence as a political and social factor, its position is not without elements of weakness. No statistics are available, but acquaintance with large groups of second- and third-generation immigrant families is likely to leave the impression that American Catholicism suffers fully as much from losses of those baptized in infancy— what Catholics refer to as "fallen aways"—as does Protestantism. Even more disturbing to the Catholic press is the dwindling number of vocations, especially in the case of nuns. As to the cause, the Catholic press does not agree. As an outsider, I suspect that the rapid increase in business and professional opportunities for American girls, taken in conjunction with the medieval discipline in most of the orders of nuns, has a great deal to do with it. So much of the church's charitable and educational program depends on the unpaid services of these consecrated women that one has no difficulty in understanding the note of desperate urgency in the many appeals and advertisements in the Catholic press for more women's vocations.

Defensive and Offensive Efforts Summarized

Now, we shall try to summarize briefly what has been said in these two chapters about the Roman Catholic Church. What is its position in the crisis of these times? It remains a great church, showing its ability to produce genuine piety and saintly living in every land where it is planted, and to sustain martyrs in their agony. "I cannot," said John Wesley on one occasion, "argue against matter of fact"—and these devout, devoted, ministering lives of saintly Catholics—priests, some of them, and laity—are matters of fact we should always bear in mind. Such lives leave their mark on even such a chaotic world as this, and we should thank God for them.

Moreover, the papal church today is finding a sort of strength in its unbending opposition to communism. It gains a sense of clear-cut mission in this opposition which helps to weld its own ranks more closely together and to make its approaches to governments and to the secular world in general less ambiguous than is frequently the Protestant approach. It is on the offensive in tackling the characteristic social and industrial problems of our time, and it has taken an intellectual position which attracts some mind-weary intellectuals and hosts of folk without intellectual pretensions who find comfort in the sentimental and ethically nondemanding adoration of the Virgin, now presented as Co-Redemptrix of the race.

However, the Roman church in many places and many respects is on the defensive. I have tried to point out some of these indications. Perhaps the greatest handicap which afflicts Catholicism in this crisis is that it is still essentially an Italian church. The present pope has tried to alter this fact, so far as he dared, but he has not changed it. Catholics outside the Latin world stress the dependence of the papacy on the U.S.A. and other American countries for financial support. Many American Catholics will tell you that the dominant Italian influence in their church will have to change, because of the change in the world situation. That may be so. It does not alter the fact that the change has not come yet. The hordes of ecclesiastics who make up the bureaucracy of the Vatican, and thus pretty nearly run the church, are overwhelmingly Italian and imbued with the traditions of conservative Italian clericalism. The College of Cardinals is still safely Italian. This ruling Italian influence, coming out of Rome's papal aristocracy and the Vatican bureaucracy, looked down its nose at the upstart House of Savoy for the seventy years of its reign. Today it looks down its nose at an ambitious non-Italian like Cardinal Spellman. I have heard far more cutting and sneering things said about Cardinal Spellman inside Catholic circles in Rome than I have ever heard in this country—and I know quite a few American Catholics who are not among the most ardent admirers of the Cardinal Archbishop of New York.

The Italianate character of the papal church may in time disappear, but I do not believe that this will happen quickly enough to rid it of this heavy handicap while the crisis of these times continues. Therefore, the more carefully one studies the current religious situation in world terms, the more one is driven to the conclusion that it is the weakness of Orthodoxy and Protestantism, rather than any increased strength of Catholicism, which sometimes makes the papal church appear to be the most vigorous organized element among the contemporary churches.

Chapter Three

The Struggles Within
Orthodoxy

WE HAVE CONSIDERED the ways in which the Church of Rome is trying to ride out the storms of this "time of troubles" in which we are engulfed. Now we shall turn to what is going on within the life and orbit of the Greek Orthodox churches.

Until quite recently we have had in this country little knowledge of or interest in the Orthodox churches. We have known in a vague sort of way that Orthodoxy exists, one of the three great branches of Christendom. We have noted the presence of Orthodox congregations in our American cities, and may even have tried to learn how to tell, by the differing designs of crosses on their steeples, whether they were Greek or Bulgarian or Russian Orthodox. But it has taken the furore in the island of Cyprus, culminating in the exiling of the Orthodox bishop to a remote island in the Indian Ocean, to awaken most of us to the importance of the part which

Orthodoxy plays in world affairs and to the possibility that in what happens to Orthodoxy in this period when the eastern Mediterranean and the Near and Middle East have become such bones of contention, giving birth to fears, the conduct of this church may have a vital relation to our own hopes of peace.

Let us take a preliminary minute or two to look at what has been going on in Cyprus, for the struggle there between the British and the Orthodox church epitomizes a great deal of Orthodox history and reveals both the strength and the weakness of Orthodoxy.

Archbishop Makarios III has been not only head of the Orthodox church on Cyprus, but ethnarch (national leader) of the Greek Cypriots. The movement for *enosis* (union) with Greece has been kept alive by the church, fanned by the church, directed by the church. (In this it has been strikingly reminiscent of the part played by the Roman Catholic Church in keeping Polish nationalism alive during the decades of Poland's partition after the Napoleonic wars.) Makarios has been a passionate Cypriot patriot, but in dealing with the British he has had a new kind of advantage for an Orthodox bishop— funds supplied by the World Council of Churches enabled him to take advanced postgraduate training in sociology, international affairs, and religion at Boston University. He thus faced the British across the negotiating table with a thorough Western training as well as complete command of the Greek Cypriot's religious *and* political loyalties. The British finally decided that there was no way to protect their stake in this last piece of sovereign territory which they hold in the eastern Mediterranean but to banish the archbishop. But many thoughtful Britishers realize that their military bases on Cyprus will never be secure while the populace is inflamed against them, and that the Cypriots will never cease to fight the British rule by every means at hand so long as their archbishop is kept in exile.

Some prominent Englishmen, notably the Archbishop of Canterbury, while deploring the banishment of Makarios, have commented that a church leader who mixes in a political matter must expect a politician's fate when he loses. True enough. But this fails to take into account that from the days of Constantine onward, Orthodoxy has always been so closely involved in affairs of state that its bishops and priests have been as much political as religious figures. It has been the strength of Orthodoxy that it has thus, in Greece and the Balkans when they were under Turkish rule, been the great agency which has kept national loyalties alive. It has been the weakness of Orthodoxy that, in countries where the government has itself favored Orthodoxy—notably Russia—the Orthodox church has been simply one branch of the government. Religion and politics have thus been inextricably mingled, and the interests of religion have been subordinated to the interests of politics.

Orthodoxy at this juncture in its history is actually involved in three major struggles. There is, first of all, the ancient struggle with Rome—never entirely at rest, and now entering on a new phase of intensity. Second, there is the struggle between the patriarchates of Istanbul and Moscow for the leadership of the Orthodox communions. This ecclesiastical struggle has become part of the "cold war," which adds to its severity and makes its outcome doubtful. Finally, there is the struggle within all the Orthodox churches outside the Russian orbit between their pro- and anti-Communist elements. This is to be seen most vividly in Orthodox church life in the United States. Let us consider these three struggles.

The Struggle Between Istanbul and Moscow

First in order of importance, though not in historical sequence, is the struggle between Istanbul and Moscow. I assume that I need not review the story of the way in which the Eastern patriarchates developed and finally split away from the See of Rome. The Great Schism, as it has been called in the West (where even we Protestants accept a nomenclature embodying a Roman historical interpretation which is repudiated by the East), took place in 1054, when Leo IX excommunicated the entire Eastern church. Despite all you read in church histories about the interminable doctrinal disputes which raged in the various church councils when the creeds were being hammered out, the break between West and East was primarily political. It left Constantinople, the Byzantine capital on the Bosphorus, the virtually unchallenged head of Eastern Orthodoxy. To be sure, the patriarchs of Alexandria, Antioch, Jerusalem, and Constantinople were recognized as equals in ecclesiastical rank. But Constantinople was the first among equals— *primus inter pares*. And the head of the church in Constantinople gradually came to assume the superior title of Ecumenical Patriarch—that is, the patriarch with the all-embracing, world-wide precedence.

However, this Ecumenical Patriarch in Constantinople soon—that is, within four centuries—found himself in the extremely disadvantageous position of living under Muslim rule and discharging his churchly office at the pleasure of what was, to him, an infidel sultan. The three other patriarchates in the East labored under the same disadvantage. To be sure, Turkish rule proved remarkably tolerant, and the Islamic despots in Constantinople in a measure built up the stature and authority of the Ecumenical Patriarch by making him their vice-regent for the government of the Christians within their empire. Nevertheless, the position of the Ecumenical Patriarch was, from 1453 on, an obviously precarious one.

Then came the appearance on the stage of world history of Russia, gradually developing, after the Mongol and Tartar invasions, from the little duchy of Moscovy into the mighty empire of the tsars. And as this empire grew in political importance, the church which had been planted in it about a century before the break with Rome likewise grew in ecclesiastical importance. There was an Orthodox metropolitan in Moscow, nominated by Constantinople, early in the fourteenth century. Later, Moscow was elevated to the dignity of a patriarchate. And as the Ecumenical Patriarch passed more and more under the shadow of the Islamic empire by whose suffrage he held office, the patriarchate in Moscow took on more and more of the rising power and prestige of the officially Christian empire in whose capital it was located. Arnold Toynbee makes a great deal of the tendency in Russian monastic circles, as early as the sixteenth century, to laud Moscow as "the third Rome."

With the modernization of Russia under Peter the Great, a drastic change took place in the organization of the Russian church. Peter did not intend to have any rival power in Moscow while he was building up his despotic rule in St. Petersburg. So he pushed the close linking of church and state which had always characterized Orthodoxy to its logical conclusion by abolishing the Moscow patriarchate and making himself the head of the Russian church, with the actual administration in the hands of a layman known as the Procurator of the Holy Synod, who was responsible directly to the tsar. This system lasted until the fall of the Romanov tsars in 1917. With the Moscow patriarchate abolished, the Ecumenical Patriarch in Constantinople was left without a rival claimant for leadership of the Orthodox churches.

Then, at the same time that Constantinople was becoming Istanbul and the Ecumenical Patriarch was finding himself residing under a Turkish lay republic which disestablished Islam and abolished the old Muslim caliphate, the Communists took over in Russia. And although they started by sequestering all church property and income, depriving priests of all civil rights and treating them with such rigor that hundreds lost their lives and thousands abjured their clerical status, and although the ruling Communist party was and remains officially atheist, the realism of Lenin and later of Stalin soon brought a restoration of church functions. The patriarchate of Moscow was restored with the blessing of the Soviet state. A toleration clause was written into the constitution that Stalin promulgated in 1936. And during World War II, when the Communist dictatorship needed to rally every possible source of popular support in Russia and its neighboring countries, when it was important to Stalin to convince his Western allies that he was one with them in spirit and ultimate purpose, the revival of the Russian church and of the Moscow patriarchate was not simply tolerated, but encouraged.

As in the case of everything behind the Iron Curtain, the materials are lacking for a satisfactory account of the present state of the Russian Orthodox Church. The report of the delegation from the National Council of Churches which recently returned from the Soviet Union is more revealing for what it leaves out than for what it says. It is known, however, that thousands of churches and scores of monasteries have been turned back by the state for religious services. There are 70 dioceses functioning, each with an average of 900 active priests—a total for all Russia of about 20,000 active churches. The civil rights of priests have been restored, they participate in public ceremonies clad in their robes of office. Though they no longer receive support from state funds and have to pay income taxes, they are permitted to charge fees on a scale which made the income of the Russian clergy, according to the delegation from the Evangelical Church in Germany which visited Russia two years ago, higher than the average clerical income in this country. For example, though the German visitors found skilled engineers—the elite among Russian workers—receiving from 1,500 to 2,000 rubles a month, priests were getting from 3,000 to 8,000 rubles, or, in terms of estimated purchasing power, up to the equivalent of U.S. $640 a month. Dr. Ralph W. Sockman, after an earlier postwar visit, estimated that the share of the higher-ranking bishops in these "voluntary" contributions for christenings, weddings, funerals, prayers for the sick and the dead, and the sale of candles for all services runs as high as the equivalent of U.S. $3,200 a month.

In return for this restoration, the Russian church has given the state important reinforcement. This came first during World War II, but it has become even more important in the "cold war" period. Under the leadership of the Patriarch Alexei of Moscow, a vigorous and intensely ambitious man, the church has stamped with its approval every development of state policy, domestic and foreign. It has been an active agent in binding the peoples of the European satellite countries to their Russian allegiance. It has been one of the main promoters of the Cominform's so-called "Stockholm Peace Appeal." It has blasted Rome as a warmonger and the World Council of Churches as a tool of Anglo-American imperialism. And it has worked incessantly to advance the interests of the Soviet Union in the Near East by arranging for the turning over of all former Russian church properties in Palestine to the Communist state and by plunging into a courtship of the patriarchates of Antioch, Alexandria, and Jerusalem. This effort has taken the Patriarch of Moscow traveling through those patriarchates, distributing decorations and honorary degrees from the University of Moscow with a lavish hand, and in turn bringing dignitaries from the area to Moscow, where they are given even more lavish entertainment than that which is proffered to church delegations from the West. This wooing of the Patriarch of Antioch seems to have been completely successful, while it has so far won the Patriarch of Alexandria as to touch off a revolt among that portion of the Orthodox clergy in Egypt who do not want their church to seem to be tied up with the interests of the Soviet Union.

Russia's Communist leaders, of course, have been as opportunistic and cynical in thus encouraging the revival of the Orthodox Church and the Moscow patriarchate as in all the other shifts of their policy. One dislikes to think what must have passed through the mind of the late dictator Stalin when he read the fawning, flattering adulation in the addresses which the church so frequently presented to him. Fortunately, the new policy which the Khrushchev-Bulganin directorate seems to be following should put an end to this sort of sycophancy, for which we have had no parallel in our part of the world since the translators wrote their address to James I as a dedication of the King James version of the Bible. But the Kremlin is continuing to use the church as an instrument of state policy, just as Romanov tsars, Byzantine emperors, and Balkan tyrants have used it for centuries. And a Communist Khrushchev, or Stalin before him, is probably no more cynical in so doing than were their Romanov forerunners. The tragedy is that the Eastern churches, since the days of Constantine, have become so accustomed to fawning on heads of state and to acting as an arm of the state (as the very word "Caesaropapism" proves) that the present role of Orthodoxy in the Soviet Union and its satellites is accepted by the church and most of the people as a matter of course.

Now this revival of the Moscow patriarchate, coupled with Russia's emergence as the greatest of European powers, has led to an attempt by the Patriarch of Moscow to seize the leadership of all Orthodoxy. That was to be expected, for the patriarchates of Jerusalem, Alexandria, and Antioch are little more than empty shells. Their patriarchs are more concerned in preserving their own status and income than with attempting to build up or shepherd their flocks. In a region of tortuously devious politics, they follow devious policies. They try to conciliate all interests and to play along with all parties. But they know that in a showdown they either pick the winner and back him or they face exile and starvation. Why wouldn't the Patriarch Alexei try to persuade these other patriarchs that Russia is to be the big winner in their part of the world, and that therefore the future welfare of Orthodoxy depends on making Moscow the ecumenical center of the Orthodox church world?

For a time it looked as though Alexei might accomplish his ambition. The 500th anniversary of the founding of the Russian church fell in 1948, and the Moscow patriarch decided to use that occasion to call an ecumenical Orthodox church council. He very nearly succeeded. He did stage an impressive church gathering in celebration of the anniversary, which brought together more high-ranking Orthodox prelates than had attended any gathering so far in this century. But at the last moment the other patriarchs refused to recognize its ecumenical status, so Alexei's ambition to be hailed as Ecumenical Patriarch was rebuffed. However, it is an ambition which he has by no means surrendered. He continues his assiduous wooing of the three other patriarchs and appears to be making headway.

The relations between the Russian Orthodox Church and other non-Roman churches cannot, however, be left here. Because Orthodoxy is always so responsive to shifts in the political situation in the countries where its churches are located, this attitude of the Moscow patriarch toward the World Council of Churches and the Protestant and Anglican communions may change as swiftly and decisively as the line of the Kremlin. The smiling protestations by Khrushchev and Bulganin of their desire for friendship is already beginning to be reflected in the hitherto frowning countenance of Patriarch Alexei. All sorts of church delegations from other countries, including a distinguished one from the United States, are being welcomed in Moscow, and Moscow is beginning to reciprocate by sending delegations of churchmen abroad. If the Kremlin ever decides that it would be a good thing for its purposes to have all Orthodoxy voting inside the World Council, then we can expect not only to have the patriarchate of Moscow

apply for membership, but to see the membership of
Antioch, Alexandria, and Jerusalem transformed from
its present nominal status in that body to active participation. Should that happen, the council would be confronted with one of its most severe tests, for it can then
be expected that it will be the Greek Ecumenical Patriarch himself who, from Istanbul, will raise the warning
cry: "Beware these Greeks bearing gifts!"

And what has happened to the Ecumenical Patriarch
at Istanbul while all this has been going on? Inevitably,
he has found his position increasingly insecure. One
after another, the Orthodox churches of Bulgaria, Ru-
mania, Albania, and, for a time, Yugoslavia cast off any
pretense of recognizing his primacy. The civil war in
Greece threatened that foundation of the Istanbul patriarchate. What might have happened had not the "cold
war" extended to the eastern end of the Mediterranean,
there is no telling. But after the Truman Doctrine announced that the United States intended to keep the
Greek-Turkish area from falling under Russian control,
a sudden change in the fortunes and prospects of the
Istanbul patriarchate followed.

What went on in that period of 1947 and 1948, no
one on the outside knows. If the secret archives of the
United States Department of State are ever opened,
some interesting revelations will undoubtedly come to
light. Now one can only guess. But in the light of events
which actually took place, one can hardly arrive at any
other hypothesis than that the United States stepped in
to checkmate the ambitions of the Patriarch of Moscow and to place a candidate of its own on the throne
of the Ecumenical Patriarch.

What is it that we actually know about the events
of those days? Simply this: that the Ecumenical Patri-

arch then reigning, Maximos V, was believed to be a weak personality, susceptible to Soviet pressure and unlikely to stand up very long before Alexei's drive to take over Orthodox leadership. So, although a comparatively young man (he was only 53), he was suddenly discovered to be in ill health, and was prevailed on to resign. Evidently this was against his personal inclination, for he fled from Istanbul and for some months took refuge in a Greek monastery. Finally, however, he was induced —by what means we do not know—to return to Istanbul and divest himself of his office.

Thereupon Archbishop Athenagoras of New York, the exarch of Orthodoxy in the United States, an American citizen who had been for eighteen years resident in this country, was elected Ecumenical Patriarch. And to make the choice as dramatic as possible, Athenagoras was then flown from New York to Istanbul in the private plane of the President of the United States, and after his enthronement presented himself to the President of Turkey as the bearer of a special message from President Truman. Throughout eastern Europe and the Near East the whole maneuver was taken to mean just one thing—that the United States had selected its own man to claim the leadership of Eastern Orthodoxy, and intended to sustain him there against the pressures and counterclaims of the Patriarch of Moscow as a matter of American foreign policy.

All this probably sounds like a queer business for the United States to be getting mixed up in. It suggests that our State Department has been doing things to affect church affairs in eastern Europe which, if it were remotely to approach doing the same sort of things in this country, could be expected to bring an uproar from the American people. The United States, we say, is

committed by its Constitution to the principle of separation of church and state, yet here it seems to be using
what look suspiciously like strong-arm methods to force
an alien nominee of its own choosing on the highest
synod of a church in another country. I shall not be
surprised if, in years to come, a flock of unwanted chick-
ens fly home to roost from this election of Athenagoras
I as Ecumenical Patriarch of Istanbul. But the "real-
ists," whether in the Orthodox Church or the State Department, will point out that the result has been a new
vigor in Istanbul and a new readiness there to battle
Moscow right down the line. Of course, if Russia should
finally take over the Middle East and the Mediterranean, if American, British, and French influence should
be forced out of that area, Moscow would then take
over the Ecumenical Patriarchate, for this is essentially
a political issue, as all issues concerning the government
of the Orthodox churches have always been, and it will
finally be politically decided. If Moscow should thus
win, however, it will know it has been in a battle.

Meanwhile, the Ecumenical Patriarch, in spite of any
support the United States or any other Western nation
can give him, is caught in the intense political crisis now
gripping the Near East and the world of the Mediterranean. His is indeed an unhappy personal situation. It
has been made increasingly difficult by the *enosis* movement in Cyprus, with its demand for a plebiscite in
which the Cypriots can vote to have their island made
a part of Greece. The driving force behind this movement comes largely from the Greek church, both on
Cyprus and in Greece. The Turks demand that if there
is to be any change in the political status of Cyprus it
shall be returned to Turkey. This tension came to a
head on the night of September 6, 1955, when mobs in

Istanbul sacked and burned numbers of Greek Orthodox churches, desecrated Greek cemeteries, destroyed
church relics of immense age and value, killed a good
many Greeks, including some priests, and beat up hundreds of others. Only the Phanar (the seat of the patriarchate, which is to Istanbul what the Vatican is to
Rome) was spared from mob destruction when Turkish troops belatedly moved in to protect it. Even though
nothing happened to the person of Patriarch Athenagoras during that night of horror, he was at least given
a stern reminder that though Greece is the core of his
patriarchate, he dare not support the policies to which
the people and the church in Greece give virtually unanimous and passionate approval without exposing himself to the possibility of mob vengeance in his Turkish
residence, or to the greater likelihood of punitive action
—either imprisonment or expulsion—on the part of the
Turkish government.

The Struggle Between the Orthodox and the Roman Catholic Churches

We come now to that ancient struggle—the struggle
between the East and the West, between the Orthodox
churches and the See of St. Peter. This can be most
readily considered, in contemporary terms, under three
heads: (1) the struggle of Moscow against Rome; (2)
the relations of Istanbul with Rome; and (3) the effort
of Rome to weaken the Orthodox strength.

I have spoken of the struggle which Rome is waging
against Moscow—that is to say, against communism,
which the Pope calls the "infernal enemy." But Moscow is just as outspoken in its condemnation of Rome.
And it is trying just as hard to undermine the position
of the papal church. Patriarch Alexei has picked up the

old disputes over church order, has pronounced Rome heretical and has declared that the Roman congregations are guilty of schism from the "one true church" of the apostles. Coupled with this dogmatic attack, however, is an even more blistering and continuous attack on the Vatican as a source for the sowing of the seeds of war and on the Pope himself as a warmonger. This is a theme which has been much broadcast from Moscow, and usually the attacks are in the name of the Russian Orthodox Church.

In return for such powerful support for its international policies, the Kremlin is helping the Orthodox church gain certain tangible advantages at the expense of the papacy. The most spectacular of these took place in 1948 in Transylvania, when the Uniate congregations with 1,700 priests and 1,250,000 members, who had been in communion with Rome, were taken over bodily into the Orthodox ranks. Communist state power was used ruthlessly to bring this to pass. Such priests as resisted—there seem to have been about 100—were sent to prison or into the exile of labor camps. Similar pressure has been exerted against Roman Catholic minorities in the other satellite countries of southeast Europe. And in Poland and Czechoslovakia, the Communists have gone to great lengths to promote the growth of the hitherto small Orthodox minorities and to confer new public importance and honors on the Orthodox bishops. The fervor of the Pope's exhortations to "the faithful" in Poland to remain true to their Roman allegiance suggests that this pressure must be growing more severe and that it must be having enough effect to worry Rome.

As to the relations of Istanbul with Rome, one cannot but wonder what the meaning is of certain acts by the Ecumenical Patriarch. Athenagoras I is, as we said, a former American citizen (he had to renounce that citizenship and become a Turkish citizen to be crowned as Ecumenical Patriarch) who came to his eminence with unprecedented public manifestations of support from the American government. The American government seems to regard the Vatican as a valuable ally in the cold war against the Kremlin; only a fear of outraged Protestant resentment has so far kept the United States government from establishing an embassy at the seat of the papal church. Does this, or does it not, have any relation to the fact that ever since Athenagoras became Ecumenical Patriarch a major concern of his has been to promote a rapprochement between Orthodoxy and the Roman church? He has spoken of this frequently, sometimes in terms which almost suggested that reunion is just around the corner. While Alexei of Moscow has castigated Rome, Athenagoras of Istanbul has wooed it. And he has indulged in several remarkable symbolic acts. Thus, on the tenth anniversary of the enthronement of Pius XII, the Ecumenical Patriarch paid a formal visit to the papal Apostolic Delegate to Turkey to offer his congratulations. Even more astonishing, on Greek Independence Day in 1949, Athenagoras actually invited the Apostolic Delegate to celebrate a Roman mass in the Greek consulate in Istanbul! One can only speculate as to whether there is any connection between the remarkable friendliness of the Ecumenical Patriarch for Rome and the fact that for the first time Turkey has established diplomatic relations with the Vatican. Whether because his rival patriarch in Moscow is at such open war with the Pope, or because his American sponsors are so friendly to the Pope, or for reasons of his own, the Istanbul patriarch certainly seems intent on making every possible effort to heal the breach between East and West. But if that is his hope, Athenagoras must have received a shock when, in 1951, the Pope, in his *Sempiternus Rex* encyclical celebrating the 1500th anniversary of the Council of Chalcedon, after calling for a union of all Christians against "the infernal enemy," proceeded to make it clear once more that this could be attained only by prior acceptance of the primacy of the papacy. Rome will never give an inch in its dispute with Orthodoxy on that issue.

Finally, account must be taken of the efforts which Rome is making to whittle away at Orthodox strength around the edges of the Orthodox world. The Pope hurls his thunderbolts at communism, while reiterating his love and concern for the people in Communist countries and frequently inviting them back into the true fold if they will but accept the papal claims. But he knows that this invitation will not be accepted. It is made, as we Americans say, "for the record." The real papal effort is what might be called a flank attack against the Nestorian and Monophysite churches that lie alongside the Orthodox patriarchates. This has taken the form of the organization of the Uniate churches— churches which have retained their own liturgy and customs (including a married clergy), but have accepted the primacy of the Roman pontiff. The first Uniate church, that of the Maronites of Lebanon, was drawn away from Constantinople as early as 1182. This effort to woo the Nestorians, or Assyrians, as they are known today, and the Monophysites—the Copts, the Armenians, the Syrians or Jacobites—has recently been stepped up, for Rome these days has something tangible to offer these hard-pressed bodies both in material resources and in a promise of powerful international protection. The main purpose of the important encyclical *Sempiternus*

Rex was to promote the campaign to bring these bodies into a Uniate reunion. It should also be noted that in Palestine the Roman church is working assiduously, if at times deviously, to secure the dominant position when a permanent political order is established at the principal shrines, thus displacing Orthodoxy in prestige.

The Struggle Between Pro- and Anti-Communists in Orthodox Churches

Lack of space precludes a discussion of the third struggle within Orthodoxy, that between the pro- and anti-Communist elements in the Orthodox churches on this side of the Iron Curtain, and especially in this country. These Orthodox churches maintain the nationalistic divisions characteristic of the Orthodox churches in the various parts of Europe from which their immigrant founders have come. They have not been assimilated into American life in the way in which Protestant churches with an immigrant background, as for instance the Lutherans, have been. Practically all these Orthodox churches except the Greek have split on the Communist issue. For this reason, they are frequently involved these days in property disputes which come before the U.S. courts.

The state of Russian Orthodoxy in the United States may be taken as roughly true of all these bodies. These Russian churches are now divided into three branches, and it takes more knowledge than most American churchmen possess to distinguish one from another. There is the Russian Orthodox Church Outside Russia, which a few years ago moved its headquarters from Germany to Lake Mahopac, N. Y. The churches in this small group, which have not recognized the authority of Moscow since 1917, are made up largely of white Rus-

sians. Then there is the large Russian Orthodox Greek
Catholic Church in America, under Metropolitan Le-
onty. This church claims a membership of almost half
a million, and it has worked its way around the Communist problem, despite heavy pressure from Patriarch
Alexei, by theoretically recognizing the *spiritual* authority of Moscow but insisting on its own complete independence in matters of administration and church government. Finally, there is the small Patriarchal Russian
Orthodox Church, which consists of less than a dozen
congregations, completely obedient to Moscow. It is this
minute church which has been given custody of St.
Nicholas Cathedral in New York City by the courts,
and whose Moscow-appointed head, Archbishop Boris—
who recently toured Canada—has been denied permis-
sion by the United States State Department to reside in
this country. While this internal struggle goes on, these
churches can hardly be expected to contribute much to
the spiritual issues of the day, except to confirm their
adherents in whatever political loyalties they already
hold.

The Relation of Orthodoxy to the World Council of Churches

The World Council of Churches is doing its best to
bring the Orthodox churches into its fellowship. Tech-
nically, all the patriarchates except Moscow are in. But
Moscow is doing its best to keep the adherence of Antioch, Alexandria, and Jerusalem from being more than
nominal, and so far has succeeded in that aim. The
Russian patriarchate charges that the World Council,
despite all its pretensions to ecumenicity, is so far under
American and British domination that it functions as
simply another arm of Anglo-American policy in the

cold war. You may remember that in one of the most unhappy episodes in the council's brief history, when—after the Communist triumph in China—the first Asian member of the five-man presidium of the World Council, Dean T. C. Chao of Yenching University in Peking, resigned, he made this same accusation that the council is a tool of Anglo-American imperialism in his letter of resignation.

Orthodox adherence to the World Council thus far has been very tentative. When the council held its organizing assembly at Amsterdam in 1948, only 24 delegates showed up to fill the 85 seats which had been allotted to Orthodoxy. And these delegates came from Greece, which Moscow dismisses as an American puppet state, or from seminaries and congregations in France, England, Canada, and the United States. It had been hoped that the professed good will of the present Ecumenical Patriarch, Athenagoras I, would secure more Orthodox representation at the Second World Assembly of the World Council, held in Evanston in 1954. The delegation there did turn out to be larger, and it took a much more active part in the proceedings. But there were no delegates from patriarchates other than Istanbul; even the Greek delegation came only at the last minute and was confined to laymen; and the Orthodox delegation seemed intent on emphasizing its differences from rather than its agreements with the other member churches in the council. As the Evanston Assembly was in its closing hours, Archbishop Michael, exarch of the Greek church in North and South America, who had been elected to the presidium of the council for the next six years, read an intransigent paper in which it was explained that the representatives of Orthodoxy, even when in associated action with other churches, could never compromise on Orthodoxy's claim to be the one and only true, catholic, and apostolic church.

What all this means is that even such restricted Orthodox participation in the World Council of Churches as has been achieved can be continued only if a gentleman's agreement is observed not to push issues in the council concerning the nature of the church and clerical orders. Or, to use the terminology of the council, Orthodoxy can continue fellowship with the Protestantism of the West in the "Life and Work" tradition of the council's interests; for the sake of all concerned it had better give a wide berth to matters of "Faith and Order." If the Orthodox churches in this country take part in the conference on "The Nature of the Unity We Seek," to be held under World Council auspices at Oberlin, Ohio, in 1957, I predict that their account of the only kind of church reunion acceptable to them will come as a shock to most American Protestants.

The Intellectual Struggle Within Orthodoxy

There is one other struggle within Orthodoxy which perhaps should be discussed—that is, the intellectual struggle. Unfortunately, there is not much of it. There is some intellectual ferment in a few spots, such as the theological seminary of St. Vladimir which was formerly in Paris and is now in New York. But even that school, which has been supported by American money and uses the facilities of Union Theological Seminary, has recently forced out its most distinguished professor, Fr. Georges Florovsky, for too much friendliness to liberal doctrinal ideas in the Western churches.

The philosophic writing of the late Nicolas Berdyaev was also a reminder that thinking in the modern vein does go on among some of the Orthodox laity, though from the standpoint of Russian church dogma Berdyaev was a hopeless heretic. The University of Athens is furnishing some intellectual stimulation and, in the West, Orthodox priests in growing numbers are studying in our universities and graduate schools of theology. The World and National Council of Churches are trying to help along this movement for awakening the intellectual life of Orthodoxy by arranging for postgraduate studies by numbers of promising young Orthodox priests in Germany, Holland, Scotland, England, and the United States. This is all to the good. Yet the low level of education among much of the Orthodox clergy, inside and outside Russia, must be recognized. The actual state of mind within these Eastern communions is fairly accurately reflected by the fact that the issue which today most stirs the Orthodox church in Greece, an issue on which about 350 priests have been sent to prison and numbers of congregations suppressed by force, is as to whether the Gregorian or the Julian calendar shall be observed!

What Orthodoxy really needs, if it is to become a determining factor in the life of eastern Europe and the Middle East during the next hundred years, is a Protestant Reformation and the separation of church and state. Both are a long way off, and any move toward either will be as bitterly fought within Orthodoxy as both such developments were fought in the West. Meanwhile, while recognizing that Orthodoxy does still produce mystics and contemplative saints in monasteries and among small numbers of priests and believers, one must conclude that the Orthodox contribution to the extension of Christian influence in the crisis of these times will not be large (1) because of Orthodoxy's ingrained subservience to political matters; (2) because so much of Orthodoxy, especially within Communist areas, is involved in a sheer struggle for survival; and (3) because what energies the Orthodox bodies have left, over and above this struggle for survival, are so largely involved in the duel between Istanbul and Moscow for ecclesiastical dominance.

Chapter Four

World Protestantism in the Crisis

I HAVE TRIED, however inadequately, to sketch the part being played in today's world situation by two great branches of Christendom—the Roman Catholic and the Eastern Orthodox Churches. Now we must ask the same questions concerning the Protestant churches. What is their present condition? And what may we expect them to contribute in the foreseeable future to the resolution of man's problems? I am dividing this inquiry into two parts. We shall look at the status and prospects of Protestantism on other continents. And then we shall conclude with a consideration of the Protestant churches in the United States.

For all thoughtful Protestant leadership everywhere this is a time of grave heart searching. Despite statistical assurances that there are more Protestants in the world today than ever before (193 million, says the *Encyclopedia Britannica*) we have no sense of growing influence. It is very seldom, and then within narrowly limited confines, that we catch a feeling that Protestantism is molding contemporary life. More often, there is a fear that our Protestant churches are becoming simply respectfully tolerated institutions in which the traditional rituals of social good form are conducted—baptisms, marriages, worship services, burials—but from which neither great light nor great leading is expected.

Protestantism in Europe

This mood of heart searching and anxiety is, we are all aware, partly the result of recent events. Especially in Europe, the life of society and of nations has taken a turn which seems to reflect a rejection of the Protestant ethic. The two world wars which have reduced so much of Europe to ruins and slaughtered the flower of the youth of two generations have not driven the people to their knees or into the churches, as we were told they would while the fighting was still going on. On the contrary, we now have millions—especially among the industrial workers and the surviving youth—indifferent to the churches when they are not contemptuous of them. A striking but incontrovertible fact about European countries which traditionally have been Protestant strongholds—such countries as England, Scotland, Holland, and the Scandinavian nations—is the almost complete withdrawal of organized labor from the churches and the rapid shrinking in the number of young people who show more than the most passive interest in Protestant church activities.

A conversation I had more than two decades ago with James Middleton, who was for years the man that really ran the machinery of the British Labor party, is pertinent at this point. Others, such as Ramsay MacDonald and Arthur Henderson, made the speeches and gathered the honors and applause, but "Jim" Middleton was the man who made the Labor party machinery turn. Ask any member of the party in the '20s and '30s. In talking with Mr. Middleton one day about Labor's rise to power I said something about the part which a religious experience had played in producing the original leaders of the Labor party, and about how many of them had been local preachers and had gained their training for political life by preaching in Wesleyan and other Nonconformist chapels. Mr. Middleton agreed that that was true, but he took violent exception to the use made of the fact by the churches to prove their influence.

"The early leaders of the Labor party," he said, "were religious men of the kind you describe. But what counts is that once the First World War, where God again turned out to be a tribal god in the churches, swept over the party, the young people who have since then been coming into the party, and who either now are or soon will be its leaders as well as its rank and file, are completely out of touch with the churches and have no interest in them." That is a sweeping generalization, but candid English ministers will agree that it is very nearly true. The most striking fact about Protestant churches in England today—and in this I include the Anglican as well as the free churches—is the emptiness of most of them. You will remember how startled Billy Graham apparently was when he first discovered this fact. And his meetings in England and Scotland have not changed it.

The situation is even more dismal, if that is possible, in Scotland than in England. And in Scandinavia it is appalling. Not only are the organized workers there out of touch with the churches—most of them as Continental Marxists accept Marx's view of religion as a fable and churches as agencies through which the exploiting possessors seek to bamboozle the exploited workers into contentment with their lot—but most other elements in the Scandinavian populations, except the aristocracy, the older farmers, and the conservative business groups, are likewise out of touch.

I recall the astonishment with which the editor of the leading newspaper in Stockholm—a man who served for a time in this country as a professor at Cornell University—looked at me when I told him that I was making a study of church conditions in Sweden. "But why?" he asked. "The church is simply a venerable old monument in Sweden. We support it for historical and sentimental reasons. But it no longer plays an important part in Swedish life. If you want to study Swedish religion to-day, go back to the United States. There are ten times as many Swedes in church any Sunday in the United States as you will be able to find in Sweden." Again that was a judgment, as I was to discover, far too sweeping and distorted. But the fact that it could be made by a man in that position, whose personal friendliness to the church was vouched for later by Swedish church leaders, is extremely significant as bearing on the present status of Protestantism in Scandinavia.

While there has been this inner seepage from the Protestant churches all over Europe, the Protestant ranks have been terribly shaken by the volcanic political events of recent years. In Germany, the birthplace of Protestantism and its European stronghold, the ordeal of Hitler and nazism has been followed by a division of the nation which has thrown the majority of Protestants into the eastern Communist state. West Germany today, so largely made up of the Catholic Rheinland and Bavaria, the Marxist Ruhr and the seaports, is a region

of Protestant weakness, not strength. Dr. Martin Nie-
möller has had far more justification for his warnings
concerning the Catholic power in West Germany than
has been generally recognized in this country.

In other parts of Europe, the spread of communism
since the war has rocked the Protestant churches. This
is conspicuously so in Czechoslovakia, the land of John
Huss. I do not know how it affects you, but to me the
sight of the great gulf which has opened between our
part of the Protestant world and a man like Professor
Hromadka of Prague is inexpressibly tragic. During the
years while Hitler overshadowed Czechoslovakia, when
Professor Hromadka was an exile in this country, teaching at Princeton Theological Seminary, he won the ad-
miration of all who came to know him. As a scholar,
his eminence was at once established. When the war
ended, Princeton offered him every possible inducement
to stay here permanently as a member of its faculty.
But he believed that his place was with his own people,
sharing their hardships as they struggled to re-establish
their nation after the years under Nazi occupation. So
we applauded his loyalty to his native land when he
went back to Czechoslovakia, where he became dean of
the John Huss theological faculty in the University of
Prague.

As the rift between the Communist and non-Com-
munist worlds has widened, with Czechoslovakia inside
the Communist Iron Curtain, Professor Hromadka has
seemed to us on this side to accept with a distressing
lack of critical objectivity the Communist claim to be
building a new social order in Europe and its charge
that the United States stands at the forefront of im-
perialist and capitalist reaction. That he sincerely believes the policies of our government to be headed in

the direction of another world war, is probably true. This explains and in a sense justifies the sweeping condemnations of American and British policies he has at times published. But it makes difficult genuine communication with him, or with the Czech Protestants whom he represents, when he attends the various sessions of the World Council of Churches. And the personal attacks on him as a suspected Communist agent, which are published in our press when he comes to Amsterdam or Evanston, or which inspired the riots that broke up the meeting at which he was to have spoken during the recent session of the World Council's Central Committee in Australia, further widen the gulf.

This sense of the opening of a great dividing gulf between them and us is true of the Protestant churches in all the other Communist countries. It made the Hungarian delegates to the Evanston Assembly of the World Council a lonely and suspected band. It has cut off virtually all contact with the Methodists of Bulgaria. And when you cross the Urals into Asia, the condition is even more disturbing. Look at what has happened to cut us off from Protestantism in China. But of that more later.

However, the sense of crisis in European Protestantism has been produced by more than the pressure of external events. In part it is also a reflection of the theological trend which has been so marked in Continental Protestantism since the First World War, which brought the emergence of Barth and Brunner—especially Barth—and the resurrection of that melancholy Dane, Kierkegaard. Of course, this theological trend, to which the name of "crisis theology" has been applied, is in itself a reflection of the events of this past half-century. Theology is always a reflection of contemporary history, little as the theologians usually know it or will admit it. To me it has always seemed that one of the most important books the late Bishop McConnell wrote—though it has received very little attention—was the one he entitled *Public Opinion and Theology*. In it he laid down the proposition, and amply proved it, that the theology of any period reflects the public opinion, the way the masses of people are thinking, in that period. I think that is obviously true of European Protestantism's present crop of crisis theologians. And it is of interest to see how, as the United States is drawn deeper and deeper into this same crisis which overwhelmed Europe in 1914, and which we fear may overwhelm us tomorrow, we are producing our own crop of crisis theologians—although we prefer to call them by some other name.

That there has been much spiritual insight in the crisis theology I am sure we are all aware. Nevertheless, the stress which it places on man's corrupted nature, his inability to extricate himself from the Pauline nightmare of doing evil when he would do good, and the illusory nature of his hope of reaching any Christian consummation within the bounds of history—all this has contributed to the loss of confidence on the part of today's European Protestantism. It was a measure of the *influence* of this type of theology that its great high priest, Karl Barth, was chosen to preach the sermon on the opening day of the first Assembly of the World Council of Churches in Amsterdam in 1948. Do you remember the text which Barth chose and the theme which he expounded? Barth's text came from Isaiah 8:10—"Take counsel together and it shall come to nought; speak the word and it shall not stand." And the sermon was a homily on the uselessness of all such human efforts as the World Council symbolized. Barth poured out his scorn even on the theme of the Amsterdam Assembly, "Man's Disorder and God's Design," saying that "from the world's disorder, and also from our Christian analyses and postulates applied to it, there is no view, no way that leads out and up to God's design." To be sure, Barth seemingly found enough value in the ecumenical fellowship at Amsterdam so that he remained to the close of the sessions. But the debilitating nature of his theological outlook was clearly indicated by that opening sermon. When to the influence of a theology of this sort you add the influence of the fundamentalistic and millenarian sects (which are much more widespread in Europe than many American Protestants realize) you have another reason for the feeling of helplessness and despair which pervades so much of European Protestantism today.

Religion everywhere today is struggling against the powerful influences of what the Germans call the Zeitgeist (spirit of the times). But nowhere is this struggle more critical than in Europe. We are all familiar with its characteristics: secularism; "scientism" (by which I mean the almost blind worship of the supposed authority of physical science); the loss of objective standards of morality under the impact of world wars. But sometimes we fail to see that they have shifted the tests applied to religion from what they were as recently as when some of us entered the ministry. Religion today is being challenged to prove, not so much that it is intellectually respectable as that it is morally relevant—relevant to the problems of nations, such as the overshadowing problem of war, and relevant to the problems of individuals, such as that of maintaining individual worth in a society which is being forced by the social and political crisis toward ever-tightening forms of collectivist regimentation. It is this problem of relevance which confronts and torments all the churches today, and especially the churches of Europe.

For European Protestantism, moreover, the situation is, I am convinced, made more rather than less difficult by the persistence of the system of state churches. I know you cannot get clergy in the various Protestant establishments to agree to this, nor indeed many in the European free churches. They continue to paint romantic pictures of the established church as the spiritual center and home of the whole community, with the parish priest or pastor the recognized shepherd of souls for the entire population of the parish, where state recognition and support is a small return for the contribution to communal solidarity, order, and morality made by the state church. There may have been some reality in this picture in Elizabethan or Puritan England, when every Englishman attended his parish church every Sunday under pain of fine if he failed to do so, and imprisonment if he failed to communicate. Today, however, the actual working of establishment is to leave countries like England and Scotland filled with churches from which the congregations have largely vanished, and Scandinavian countries—especially Sweden—involved in a constant political battle over the prerogatives of the state churches and clergy. The clergy of the Scandinavian state churches are everywhere fighting a dogged rearguard battle to hang on as long as possible to the legal forms which the masses of the people resent as immoral infringements on the rights of conscience and their personal liberties.

Yet a church which has known the financial backing of state establishment cannot contemplate the uncertainties of voluntary support without apprehension, and hence will fight to retain its privileged position long after it has lost the sympathy of the working masses. The late Archbishop Temple once said to a friend of mine that there was just one topic which could be counted on to draw a full attendance at the convocation of his archdiocese. That was disestablishment. Suggest that, even as a topic for discussion, and you were stretching forth an impious hand to touch the sacred ark. Those of you who have been watching the postwar experiences of German Protestantism must have noted how the EKD—the postwar Evangelical Church formed out of the Lutheran and Reformed Churches—has been trying to rid itself of all control by the state while still hanging on to the financial benefits of tax support.

Even in countries which have come under Communist rule, if established Protestant churches have survived at all (as they have not, for instance, in the Baltics), there is still this attempt to retain government support. Witness the elaborate treaties—for that is what they amount to—made with the Communist governments of Czechoslovakia and Hungary. These Communist governments are glad to continue the old financial assistance, for it helps to insure a Protestantism which will not make trouble for the regime. The relation between these subsidies granted by the Communist states and the support given by the churches to the Communist governments seems so clear to us that we wonder why it does not undermine the whole theory of state-supported churches in the eyes of other European Protestants. But it does not do so, as has been shown whenever questions of church order have come up in the Assemblies, sectional meetings, or central committee meetings of the World Council of Churches.

This brings me to another question: what about the part being played by the free churches in Europe? It is an important part. In some countries—especially those of Scandinavia—the free churches provide almost the sole surviving link between Protestantism and the laboring masses. In Germany, the free churches, though comparatively small in number, are rendering a ministry of constantly rising importance. Should the EKD fall back into the stereotyped pietism of the old Lutheranism—something that seems to be growing more possible all the time—the free churches in Germany will be Protestantism's greatest hope for the future. Yet it needs to be recognized that many of these free churches are intensely conservative, even fundamentalistic, in their theology, and that they preach a literalistic interpretation of Scripture which plays directly into the hands of the Communist propagandist with his assertion that religion is antiscientific and a refuge for superstitious and belated minds. This is strikingly true of the Baptist Churches in Russia, although we are constantly referred to those churches as evidence of the vitality of religion which survives in the Soviet Union.

This is as good a point as any at which to call attention to a habit we have which frequently distorts our accounts of the church and Christianity. This is our tendency to interpret the church to the world as though the particular kinds of churches with which we are identified are normal for the whole. We say, "The church stands for this and this," or "Christianity teaches thus and thus," when what we really mean is that liberal American Protestant free churches stand for these positions. We forget that there are such things as the Roman Catholic Church, the Eastern Orthodox churches, the European state churches, and fundamentalist churches and sects by the hundreds—a total church constituency bearing the name Christian which far outnumbers that in the kind of churches we are talking about. We tend to deceive ourselves, and to involve ourselves in an effort, however innocent, to deceive others, by this slipshod manner of speaking. Yet we do it all the time. I can refer you to many examples in the editorial columns of *The Christian Century* for the years during which I was editor of that paper.

I must not leave this consideration of the present state of European Protestantism without making a brief reference to one postwar development which bears great promise. This is the rise of lay movements, such as are coming out of conference centers like Sigtuna in Sweden, the "Church and World Institutes" which Professor Hendrik Kraemer launched in Holland, the gatherings at Bad Boll and some dozen other conference centers in Germany and at the Ecumenical Institute at Boissy near Geneva in Switzerland, and the tremendous gatherings of German Protestants at the biennial Kirchentag rallies under lay leadership in both West and East Germany. To a large extent these represent a response to the loss of clerical leadership inflicted by the war. In some instances they are also a reflection of the conclusion to which some concerned Christian laymen have come, namely, that the clerical leadership of the European churches is incapable of reaching the minds of intellectuals and socialistic workers who have been deeply bitten by what Walter Lippmann calls "the acids of modernity."

All these efforts are still in their formative stages. But they hold out a real hope that if the organized churches of European Protestantism fail to make any deep impression on the contemporary crisis, there may be com-

panies of dedicated Christian laymen who will find the
way to mediate a gospel capable of arresting the attention of men caught in the ordeal faced by the church
and commanding their loyalties.

Protestantism in Asia

So much for the present state of European Protestantism. What I have said is utterly inadequate as to de-
tails, but I believe that it gives a fair picture of the total
situation and mood of Protestantism on the Continent.
Now let us look briefly at Protestantism in Asia. Here
we jump into the middle of that baffling problem—the
future of missions. It has become a cliché to say that
we are at the end of an era of colonialism throughout
Asia. But the Bandung Conference in the spring of 1955
showed how true that cliché is. And this means that we
are rapidly approaching the end of the sort of missions
—what we used to call *foreign* missions—we have known.
For missions after the traditional pattern, with missionaries sent from Western lands, supported by Western
funds, seeking to establish not only churches closely
patterned after Western models but other agencies for
the spreading of Western ideas and culture, too often
have seemed to be a sort of religious colonialism. When
all colonialism ends, as it soon will, what will be the
effect on the Protestant churches which the missions
have developed?

I cannot tell you, and I do not believe that any living
person can now be sure. But I *expect* that the effect is
going to be much more far-reaching than our missionary societies have so far grasped—or perhaps I should
say than they have publicly acknowledged. The com-
pleteness with which Christian missions have been swept
out of China and the swiftness with which an independ-

ent India has moved to place drastic restrictions on missionary activities indicates that over much of Asia for the next few decades the Protestant churches—and the Roman Catholic likewise—are going to be more concerned with the problem of sheer survival than with any expansionist efforts. It is only in the Philippines that Protestantism at present is showing any significant impulse to reach out to new fields, and I do not need to remind you that the political situation in the Philippines differs vastly from that elsewhere throughout Asia.

I shall not comment on what is happening to Protestant missions and churches in Iran, Indonesia, Burma, Thailand, Ceylon, or Korea. Let us confine our attention to Japan, China, and India. What about the state of Protestantism in those three countries?

For the first few years after the war, while the American occupation continued, we were told that Japan presented the greatest opportunity for expansion Christianity had faced in Asia for generations. Even General MacArthur joined in that assurance. But now that Japan has regained a measure of sovereignty, talk of that kind is no longer heard. The drift away from Shintoism and Buddhism, so striking in Japan immediately after the war, has stopped, and the tide of mass pilgrimages is flowing back to the shrines of those faiths. If the opportunity ten years ago was as inviting as we were told, then the present state of affairs indicates that we missed it. Why? I should like to suggest three reasons:

1. The Japanese Protestant church after the war found itself so involved in internal stresses and strains that it had little energy left for reaching out to make converts. The Kyodan (the United Church of Christ in Japan) which had come together under government

pressure during the war, has been so snarled up in disputes over what theological formulas are or are not required, and has been so shaken by the withdrawal of churches that have professed dissatisfaction with its orthodoxy or its conception of church order, that it is spending most of its strength just on keeping from falling apart entirely. On the other hand, the churches which have seceded from the Kyodan (with the exception of the Anglicans) are so committed to a literalistic, even fundamentalistic, interpretation of the Bible and the gospel that they cannot reach the students who make up the bulk of the spiritually accessible Japanese today.

One aspect of Japanese Protestantism which is puzzling to the outsider is the contrast between the reports which come year after year of throngs at the meetings of Japanese and Western evangelists, with thousands of cards signed expressing an interest in becoming Christians, and the very slow growth of the Kyodan church. In many years there is almost no growth at all. What is the explanation? In large part, I think it is that the Kyodan is so occupied with these internal struggles of which I have just spoken that it offers no attraction to a modern-minded young Japanese who may be quite sincere in his desire to follow Christ. When Professor Brunner was in Japan, as a professor at the International Christian University, he testified that he found of most interest the so-called "no church" Christians—the Japanese who claim that they are followers of Christ but who do not join any of the existing churches. Most of them are college professors or students, or Japanese prominent in public life.

2. We must also admit that another reason for failure to bring any large number of Japanese into Christian

fellowship during the period after the surrender when so many seemed spiritually at sea was the failure of Western Protestant churches at that time to provide missionary reinforcement for the hard-pressed Kyodan on anything approaching the scale of Protestant missionary effort before the war. Even the most important postwar Protestant venture, the Japan Christian International University, was launched in a hesitant, bungling fashion, with Japanese supporters for long periods left to fear that the Western churches were not going to make good on their share of the enterprise, and to this day our backing has never reached the level which the need and the opportunity calls for. The Japan Christian International University is one of the very few major constructive missionary ventures to be launched in any part of the world since the close of the Second World War. It is a going concern, of the first importance for the future of Protestant Christianity in Japan and Eastern Asia. But our inability to recognize a real opportunity when one comes along has doomed this University to struggle along on a shoestring when it should have been made—and still should be made—one of the major projects of world Protestantism.

3. It is not pleasant to say, but it must be said, that Japan Protestantism is suffering from the reaction to the American occupation and to popular fear in Japan of American policies in the Far East. Much of the mass interest in Christianity reported in the first months after the war was really interest in America—American customs, American culture, American religion. In those days nearly everybody in Japan wanted to get on the American bandwagon. This was particularly true of the students, who were disillusioned with the old ruling groups who had led the nation to disaster. And on the

whole the American occupation was probably as popular as a military occupation could ever hope to be. (Our own Southern states, which once experienced a military occupation, are aware of just how genuinely popular any such occupation can ever be.)

But the situation has changed radically. The occupation is supposed to be over, but large detachments of American forces remain in Japan, and often their demands for more land—taken from farmers in a volcanic country where only 15 per cent of the land surface is cultivatable in the first place—feed anti-American feeling. Far more resentment has been aroused by our H-bomb experiments, not only because of the unlucky effect which our first Eniwetok explosion had on the crew of a Japanese fishing vessel and on the fishing catch which is basic to Japan's diet, but even more because of the general fear that our policies are moving toward a renewal of war on the Asian mainland, in which Japanese manpower will be called on to supply the bulk of the land forces and Japanese cities will be leveled by Communist nuclear bombs. Add to this the disillusionment of large portions of the student population at the reversal of American policy which, after putting pressure on Japan to write a constitution totally renouncing war and declaring that Japan would never again maintain a large army and navy, now is pressing for rapid Japanese rearmament, with a return to the hated conscription system. To these students, this about-face in American policy is evidence of our hypocrisy in international affairs, and they say it shows that our word is no more to be trusted than that of the Communists. Accordingly, everything connected with America is held in scorn—and that includes our religion.

These are powerful factors. Others less powerful but none the less influential could be mentioned. Taken together, they indicate, I think, that there will be no great Protestant ingathering in Japan in our generation. The door of opportunity has swung shut. Or, to change the figure, the signs multiply that we have missed the boat.

What is one to say about China? It would be easy to discuss at great length about the situation which Protestantism faces in Communist China, and still leave the subject only partially covered. I do not need to tell you that the Protestant missionary enterprise in China is, at least for our generation, at an end. Neither do I need to say that there is every reason to expect that for the next decade or longer the Protestant churches, even though entirely in the hands of Chinese Christians, will be fighting for existence. There is some evidence that in some places these churches are showing more vigor than characterized them before the Communists took over. But their effort to convince the political authorities that they are not part of an American, or Western, fifth column, but that they are as patriotically Chinese as any other portion of the population, has involved them in a public repudiation of all their old ties with the churches of the West which makes any future relinking of those ties exceedingly doubtful. One can only affirm belief in the reality of the Christian faith held by most of the Chinese Christians, and pray that God will sustain and grant them wisdom to bring the church through what is certain to be a time of great testing and frequent torment.

Recent years have witnessed some developments of great promise in Indian Christianity. The access of spiritual energy which has revitalized the non-Roman Syrian churches—the indigenous Mar Thoma churches of the Malabar coast—has been felt throughout India's Protestantism. The union of Anglican, Presbyterian, English Methodist, and Congregational elements in the United Church of South India (the only union of its kind anywhere in the world) and the possibility of a similar, perhaps even more inclusive, union in North India, has given Protestantism another increase of vigor and hope. But more recently, the upsurge of nationalistic pride, coupled with resentment against any seeming form of control or dictation from outside—a natural consequence of independence—has brought sharper attacks on the missionary enterprise in India than it has ever known. So long as Mr. Nehru's government remains in control, it is predictable that the guarantees of religious liberty in the new Indian constitution will be respected. But even the Nehru government has been forced to impose restrictions on the number of Christian missionaries who will be admitted to India and on the work those who are admitted will be permitted to do. One does not need to posit a Communist triumph in India—although that is by no means out of the question—to foresee that if Nehru's strong hand should be removed there might follow such an upsurge of anti-Christian agitation, fostered by fanatical Hindu parties, as would lead to the same kind of general expulsion of missionaries as has taken place in China. As for the prospect of aggressive evangelistic expansion led by Indian Christians, the Indian Christian community today feels under such pressure that it devotes most of its attention simply to trying to insure that state authorities give it the protection promised in the constitution. The thing it most wants, it frequently appears, is to be let alone.

Protestantism in Africa

Of the other aspects of world Protestantism, space remains for only a brief reference to the situation in Africa. There the conditions to note are three: (1) the rapidly growing churches in Central Africa, where Bishop Neale, of the World Council of Churches, reports that thousands of would-be members are being kept out of the churches because no trained ministry is available to instruct and shepherd them; (2) the question as to how long this state of affairs will continue if the color issue continues to increase in intensity, and if Christianity becomes identified in native thinking with the determination of whites to hold the desirable land and maintain political rule, while Muslim missionaries proclaim that there is no distinction of color within the brotherhood of Islam; and (3) the situation in South Africa, where strongly rooted churches are caught in the tense racial struggle that is being fomented by the policies of the Nationalist government.

World Protestantism's failure to provide a native ministry in central Africa, either large enough in numbers or well-enough educated to care for all those who seek church membership, is an old story. The trouble for the churches being compounded by white pre-emption of good land and white political control has been revealed in the Mau Mau uprising in Kenya. I wonder whether it is still sufficiently realized in the West that the Kikuyu, the tribe which produced the Mau Mau desperadoes, has been the tribe most responsive to Christian evangelism in Kenya. For the present, the Mau Mau horror is about ended, but among thoughtful observers of Central Africa there is general agreement that if there are not radical changes in the land and political policies of the ruling Kenya whites, trouble will certainly break out again. Southern Rhodesia, in the newly formed Central African Federation, is one of the few spots in Central Africa where action is being taken that is sufficiently intelligent and sufficiently rapid to hold out hope of heading off this coming trouble. For the Christian cause throughout this part of the continent, the outlook is made more problematical by the recent great increase in Muslim missionary activity. Islam is sometimes anything but gentle in its dealings with unbelievers, but once you are inside the company of those who acknowledge Mohammed as the great prophet of Allah, the one god, whatever your color or condition you experience the brotherhood that we Christians too often only talk about.

As to South Africa, where apartheid (segregation) is official policy and the dominant church, the Dutch Reformed, backs the Nationalist party in everything it does to keep the black man in his place as a hewer of wood and drawer of water, there is every reason to fear that unless that church changes its views (a few daring souls within it are calling for such change, but so far they are less heeded than are those who oppose segregation policies in the South of the United States) Protestantism will become, in the eyes of the native population, a religion which preaches that the black man is doomed, by the will and word of God, to be forever inferior and subservient to the white. Other churches in South Africa—Anglican, Protestant, and Roman Catholic—have stood out against the Nationalist policies. Some Anglican protests have been notable, but it has been only the Roman Catholic Church which, faced by the government's demand to turn its schools into the low-grade schools required by the notorious Bantu Education Act, has refused and raised the money by a world-wide appeal to Catholics to continue its schools without government subsidy as independent enterprises. If we wish to get a sense of the racial storm into which Protestantism in South Africa is heading, all we need to do is to read Alan Paton's novel—one of the few truly great novels so far written in this century, *Cry, the Beloved Country*. Should Protestantism become identified in the black man's mind with white racialism in South Africa, a Protestant country, the effect on its future in all other parts of the black man's continent will be lamentable.

The Birth and Growth of the Ecumenical Movement

This may seem like a dismal picture I have been sketching of the present condition of Protestantism on these other continents. What is there to offset it? I have already mentioned two things—the new release of lay energies in some parts of European Protestantism and the bold venture shown in the formation of the United Church of South India. It should also be recorded that many of the churches and congregations which passed through the fiery afflictions of the Nazi occupations and of war have come out with a greater sense of solidarity, a deeper piety, and a more intense religious loyalty than they have known for generations. In some countries—notably Germany—there are more young people *seeking* in the churches than there have been for many years; what they are *finding* it is too early to say. But of course the overarching development of recent years for these Protestant churches has been the birth and rapid growth of the ecumenical movement.

It is still only some forty years since the first ecumenical gathering at Edinburgh. That initial impulse to join hands resulted from the discovery on mission fields of the folly—indeed, the sin—of remaining divided in the face of the hordes of non-Christians. It gathered to itself all sorts of interests, such as the "Faith & Order" and "Life & Work" movements. Over a span of three decades, tormented by two world wars, while humanity's need for a global integration was being mocked by all sorts of divisive forces, this movement alone showed its power to transcend the boundaries of nations and bring men of different colors, different nationalities, and widely different creeds and churchly traditions, together in a common fellowship. It is a historical miracle, nothing less, that the weak, faltering, scarcely born World Council of Churches, which entered the war year of 1939 with 52 churches in its membership, came out of the war in 1945 with that number increased to 90, and today has 164 different communions, located in 47 different countries, on its roster.

One must not exaggerate the influence of the World Council. It is still, as its name avows and despite the charges sometimes made by our fundamentalist brethren, simply a *council*. That is to say, it is a body in which churches of widely differing sorts meet to consult on their mutual problems and to see whether they can find ways of working together at tasks for which, separately, they lack sufficient strength. In the effort to bring along together elements as far apart as, for instance, the Orthodox Church of Greece and the American Baptist Convention, the World Council must proceed with great caution. It must find ways of linking the "activism" of American Protestantism with the pietism and sometimes the Erastianism of European Protestantism. It must be on guard lest a semblance of justification be lent to Moscow's charge that it is a tool of Anglo-American imperialism. It must try to make fel-

lowship between the churches of Occident and Orient
a living thing. And, it must keep trying to find a recon-
ciliation between what seem utterly irreconcilable conceptions of the nature of the church, of the sacraments,
of church government and orders.

Some of us will undoubtedly grow impatient at times
at what seems the World Council's slow rate of progress. But progress there is. Protestant churches have now
been held together in Christian fellowship by it through
one period of world war. Today the lines of fellowship
are not being completely severed by an iron curtain or
a cold war, although we must admit that there is as
much difficulty in maintaining even a semblance of
fellowship between Geneva and Prague or Budapest as
there was during the war between Geneva and Berlin.
Contact between Geneva and Peiping has been all but
entirely severed. What would happen to the World
Council if another world war, the First Atomic War,
should sweep the earth, no man can know. But if humanity itself survived that catastrophe, and if the
churches thus survived, I have faith to believe that the
fellowship of the World Council would survive, and
that it would prove one of the instrumentalities by
which the postwar chaos could be challenged and finally overcome.

In the light of the desperate need of humanity today
for more wisdom than now informs the policies of governments and social institutions, I think that any careful
and candid observer must be more oppressed with a
sense of Protestantism's insufficiencies than impressed
with its achievements. That is as true for American
Protestantism, of which I shall speak in my closing
chapter, as for the Protestantism of Europe, Asia, Africa, and Australasia. But the picture is not wholly black.

There are elements of hope. There are the saving remnants, as has been shown in every Protestant church which has come under the harrow of persecution and destruction during these past thirty years. There is the continuing Protestant capacity for self-criticism, with its attendant hope of reformation. There are the little flames of new evangelism which burst out here and there, especially among laity who suddenly awaken to a realization that their religion, their faith, is their only hope. And there is the gaining power of the ecumenical movement, which is proving that barriers of nation and race and creed can be surmounted and that, even in this time of troubles, even in these days of darkness and great fear, men can reach out across all barriers to grip the hands of their Christian brothers, and so lose some of their terror and gain a new courage to preach the Lordship of Jesus the Savior to other men who are now stumbling blindly on the road to damnation.

Chapter Five

American Protestantism in the Crisis of These Times

In talking to European churchmen who have traveled in the United States, I find that they are usually impressed by the large part which the Protestant churches play in the public affairs of this country. Sometimes they argue that this is really an illusion; that we actually do not have much more influence on what goes on in this nation than they have, but that we manage to make a good deal more noise about what we do—or attempt to do—than do they. I remember a talk I once had with Dr. J. H. Oldham, the "grand old man" of British Protestantism, who explained the difference between the way in which a council of churches in the United States and a similar British body would go about trying to influence a proposed piece of legislation before Congress or Parliament.

"In your case," said Dr. Oldham, "a department of your National Council would get out a statement, the executive committee of the Council would meet and adopt a resolution, appeals would be made to hold mass meetings in a hundred cities, word would go down the line to have church members write their senators and representatives, publicity by the bushel would be fed into the mails and the newspapers, and finally a committee of bishops and other church dignitaries would be sent to Washington to see the President, the Secretary of State, and influential members of both houses of Congress, and to make sure that the wishes of the churches were given the largest possible exploitation in your press. Over here in England," he went on, "we don't work that way at all. If our British Council of Churches should see something coming up in Parliament on which it wished to express an opinion, after making sure in private discussion in the executive committee of the Council what that opinion was, the Archbishop of Canterbury, or the Bishop of Chichester, or someone like that would arrange to have lunch at his club with the Prime Minister, or the member of the cabinet in charge of the proposed legislation. There the matter would be discussed in private, an agreement reached one way or the other, and that would be that. There would be nothing in the papers, no mass meetings and no public evidence of any kind that the churches had taken a hand in public affairs. But I am not sure that our way is not as effective as yours, though by no means so spectacular. And sometimes it is just possible that it may be more effective."

There is much to be said for the English method, although it ignores the importance of educating the general church constituency which, on most public issues, is as much needed as educating a Prime Minister or members of Parliament. To most European churchmen it *does* seem that the American churches have a far greater influence on national affairs than they have been accustomed to at home. Until very recently, many Continental Protestants have inclined to scorn this as a manifestation of the American "activism" which they have dismissed as being an evidence of lack of spiritual depth. Some still do so. But the tradition against participation in public affairs by the churches is dying in European Protestantism. The ease with which Hitler set up his pagan Nazi rule in the land of Luther taught a lesson. Europe's Protestant churches are still a long way from acting on public matters as directly and as continually as do those in this country or in Canada. It was noticeable, however, that many of the European delegates to the Evanston Assembly of the World Council of Churches in 1954 went home with their scorn for American church "activism" much lessened. Bishop Berggrav of Norway reflected a widespread impression when, on his return to Oslo, he said in a broadcast that the two things in the United States which most impressed him were American kitchens and American churches.

Relative to the situation in European Protestantism, Protestantism in this country is much more vigorous—perhaps not intellectually, though I am by no means as overawed by the work of British and Continental theologians as some Americans seem to be. But in other respects the contrast is striking, for instance, in the matter of churchgoing. You may think that far too many church members in this country are lax in their church attendance, and that is sadly true. Nevertheless, there is far more general churchgoing here than you will find in any part of Europe except a few regions in Germany.

Church membership here, which credited a total of 97 million in churches of all sorts, including Jewish, as of last year, is away beyond that proportionately in the countries of Europe, except in those with established churches where, unless a person goes through a legal process of having his name removed from the parish register, he is counted as a member of the state church, no matter how estranged from it he may be. American Protestant bodies are credited with 59 million members of the world's Protestant total of 193 million—nearly one-third. It is claimed that such church statistics as we have, show that membership in American Protestant churches is growing at a faster rate than the national population, although Professor Winthrop S. Hudson of Colgate-Rochester Divinity School has recently challenged that claim with an impressive analysis of the statistics on which it is based.

None of us, I presume, are too much impressed by statistics. We know that the question of the relation of American Protestantism to the present state of the world must be answered at a deeper level than statistics —even if the statistics were reliable (which church statistics notoriously are not). But we should have added cause for concern if the statistics showed that our churches were losing membership. Much of the same thing can be said about our gifts for the support of church enterprises, of missions, of philanthropies at home and overseas. The tradition of voluntary support for all such undertakings has bred the habit of giving into our Protestant people, and although on occasion we mourn because our gifts are not larger per capita, the total is very large and argues for a considerable degree of vitality in our congregations.

Problems of Institutional Maintenance

To be sure, American Protestantism is moving into a period when problems of institutional maintenance are going to make a lot of trouble. Where we are coming out, for example, on the question of denominational colleges I do not know. Expenses for conducting worthy schools are rising as fast as income from endowment is falling. Many educators say that the only way to insure sufficient income for a first-class nonstate institution, unless the government provides scholarships for as many boys after their draft service as it did for GI veterans of the Second World War and the Korean War, is either to have some sort of army, navy, or airforce training corps stationed on the campus or to have subsidies from the armed services for doing scientific research in the college laboratories.

Many church college presidents see the peril in such arrangements. Secretly they probably had a good deal of sympathy for the remark attributed to Robert Maynard Hutchins when he resigned as chancellor of the University of Chicago—that he had no interest in continuing as head of a glorified munitions factory. They know that the glory of the church college, its best claim for support, lies in its independence, and that with the government putting up the money this independence is in peril. Accordingly, they have welcomed recent efforts to obtain funds from industrial corporations. In most states the church colleges, Catholic as well as Protestant, are now banded together in pursuit of such corporation gifts, and each year sees an impressive increase in such gifts. Yet there is a danger here also, for these corporations are interested in the church colleges mainly as a source of the trained scientists and executives they need, which means that perhaps insensibly, but none the less inescapably, these colleges will be under pressure to fashion their curricula to turn out the chemists, the physicists, the engineers, the graduates in business administration for whom American industry is so hungry.

Much the same thing applies to the cost of conducting church philanthropies such as hospitals. Government aid is now being offered for these institutions, but so far as I know the Southern Baptists are the only denomination which has consistently refused it. The more the program of American Protestantism becomes institutionalized, and the higher the cost of supporting great institutions goes, the greater will be the temptation to look to government for support. That this can be done while maintaining inviolate the principle of separation of church and state is very doubtful, and it is still more doubtful that it can be done while maintaining the prophetic role of the church as the conscience of the state. There is sufficient vigor in almost all forms of American Protestantism today to show that we have no reason to despair of the future. But the more closely one examines the situation under the surface, and particularly in this field of our institutional policies, the more cause one finds for serious concern.

The Changing American Social Scene

In many respects, the condition of American Protestantism and the part it is playing in our contemporary situation reflects what is happening to America as a whole. Protestantism formed the basis of American culture in the days when the United States was predominantly agricultural. But this situation has been changing ever since 1890, which, as Frederick J. Turner pointed out in his historic essay, was the year when the frontier officially vanished. Since then, the nation has rapidly become urbanized and industrialized. The process is speeding up as the farms become more mechanized. And it has at last begun to penetrate the South in full force.

Well, urban civilization is not Protestant. Our cities have been great catch-alls for immigration, and most of that has not been Protestant. Moreover, rural dwellers who move to the cities and go into our gigantic factories and mills, while living in the rabbit warrens of our apartment house districts, often lose touch with the church. Labor union members are not as cut off from the churches by conviction as is frequently the case in Europe—especially in Marxist Europe—but their church membership, if they maintain it, is frequently very nominal. Like many other American males, they tend to keep their religion in their wives' names.

The reverse side of this picture is to be seen in the South, which is still predominantly Protestant. Protestantism is still a mighty and a direct force in most of the South, as the Democratic party found out when it nominated Al Smith in 1928. But this is in large measure because the South has received a relatively small proportion of our immigration and is only now beginning to cast off its predominantly rural character and become as industrialized as the rest of the country. Note how, as this process goes on, the rift between such factory workers as are being unionized and the Protestant churches in the South is widening. There was very little contact between the striking workers and the churches, for instance, while the sugar strike of 1955 was on in Louisiana. Southern Protestantism, with only a few exceptions such as the Conference of Southern Churchmen (which is widely charged with being what Churchill calls crypto-Communist), usually lines up in current labor struggles on the side of the present wielders of power. That is the comfortable course for the present. But the outcome of the struggle is inevitable. The South is going to be industrialized and it is going to have organized labor exerting as much power here twenty years from now as it does today in the rest of the country. And when that day comes Southern Protestantism may have reason to regret its present course. The Roman Catholic Church is more farsighted.

American culture, in this urbanized period into which we have moved, is no longer Protestant. It has never been, and is not now, Roman Catholic. It is not religious at all. We still like to employ religious symbols, but actually we are now living in a secular culture. Secularism has taken over in the United States. By secularism I mean an outlook on life which is riveted exclusively on this world. It denies that life has any meaning beyond our immediate experience in the here and now, or if it does not make this outright denial it dismisses the question as of no importance. The extent to which this secularistic outlook has taken over can be seen by the way in which we have tossed the lore of religion out of the education we provide for our children, by the way in which we have adopted what can be called "scientism" as our substitute religion, believing that ultimate truth is to be found with calipers and test tubes and even—God save the mark!—IQ tests. It can be seen in the way in which we have surrendered to material standards of success. One sees it in the tinsel and glitter and sordidness of the commercialized amusements which bulk larger and larger in our lives. Nor is that sort of thing confined to Hollywood. It runs all through our contemporary American society. There have even been

church colleges which have sold their souls for the sake
of a bowl-winning football team. And some of the cur-
rently popular types of preaching come perilously close
to the blasphemy of promising success in the market-
place or an easy resolution of life's crises as a reward for
calling upon God. It is far too easy to promote a church
boom by telling ambitious men and women that they
can make God serve them, rather than by holding up
the demand of true religion that they shall serve God.

One factor which, I believe, tends to weaken the hold
of Protestantism and to produce an American public
without vital religious interests is our inveterate habit of
migration. I have recently been in Florida, which is being overrun these days by a Yankee horde, so perhaps
I feel this at present with peculiar sensitivity. We talk
about the migrations of our fathers, which took this
continent away from the Indians. But thanks to Henry
Ford and his imitators, the American people are more
mobile today than ever. Hermann N. Morse, who is
Protestantism's leading authority on such matters, says
census figures show that 70 per cent of all American
families move at least once every decade! The implication of social rootlessness behind such a fact is stagger-
ing. How can Protestantism put its stamp deeply on a
people who are here today and gone tomorrow?

This rootlessness also enters into the dilemma of the
suburbanized church. Protestantism's strength, at least
in and around our large northern and midwestern centers of population, increasingly is to be found in suburban churches. In the Chicago area, for example, there
are only a few Protestant churches left in the city which
command much attention. The "big" churches—and
you will understand the sense in which I use that ad-
jective—are in Oak Park, Evanston, Winnetka, and

Lake Forest. It is so in nearly every metropolitan center. But the suburban church suffers from two things:

First, there is the tendency to regard participation in the suburban church a matter of social good form, and to apply to it the same standards of success as obtain in the business and professional circles from which its members come. One of the deft touches in John P. Marquand's novel, *Sincerely, Willis Wayde*, which is the picture of a young American bound to rise by whatever means to the top of the business ladder, is the way in which Mr. Marquand has Wayde, when he makes his first big move upward and buys a house in a New Jersey suburb, join a church and become a solicitor in the every member canvass. Willis Wayde is a complete secularist without the vaguest glimmering of what the Christian religion is all about. But he knows that the up-and-coming young executive, moving into a suburban community of other up-and-coming young executives, is expected to be identified with a Protestant church.

The second problem the suburban church faces in dealing with our Willis Waydes is that in these days of giant corporations with plants and branch offices decentralized all over the nation, these young executives are seldom allowed to stay more than two or three years in a community. The suburban church rarely has time enough to make any deep impression on their lives. It is glad to have their help in meeting its heavy financial costs, but it has to accommodate itself to the knowledge that this year's chairman of the successful budget-raising campaign will next year likely be in a church a thousand miles away.

One more word about the changing American social scene and its relation to Protestantism. What about the rural America which remains? There are still farms in this country and farmers on them. Not everybody has gone to the city; it still takes at least one man to run a tractor, and electric milking machines are not yet self-attaching and -detaching. Does Protestantism retain its old hold on the farms—on that 43 per cent of our population that is still in towns of less than 2500 or in the open country? Well, except in those rural areas where the farms are passing into the hands of immigrants or of the second-generation sons and daughters of immigrants, it largely does. But even we city dwellers must be aware of the somber note in the speeches and articles of our church rural life specialists. And as the family-size farm finds itself in increasingly unfavorable economic straits, driving its children to the cities and speeding up the trend toward selling out to great holdings which are in reality farm industrial corporations, this former citadel of Protestant strength becomes progressively weaker. Many church executives will say that we have already reached a point where rural America is more of a problem than a source of strength to Protestantism.

So I suggest that there are these changing elements in American life which must be borne in mind when one tries to assess the present state of American Protestantism: our urbanization and industrialization, now spreading even across the South; our increasing secularism; our rootlessness; the middle-class nature of most of Protestantism, today being thrown into strong relief by the increasing role of our suburban churches, and to be seen in contrast to our limited contacts with the rising powers of organized labor; and the dwindling influence of the country church as the family farm loses ground in its struggle for survival and as the American rural community loses its onetime homogeneous character.

Unchanging Characteristics of the American Religious Situation

There are, however, certain characteristics of the religious situation in this country which have a long history behind them and do not reflect recent changes in our society. Most important, perhaps, is the whole conception of religious liberty, with its corollary principle of separation of church and state which has grown up under the First Amendment to the Federal Constitution and the supporting articles written into almost all state constitutions. Thomas Jefferson, George Mason, James Madison, and the others who wrote our Bill of Rights knew what they were doing when they put this charter of religious freedom in the very first clauses of the First Amendment. At that time there were established churches in certain states (the last state church was not disestablished in Massachusetts until 1834) and there had been established churches in most of the recently emancipated colonies. With Europe's experience in mind, and knowing that numbers of men had already been imprisoned on this continent and a few even put to death for lack of religious conformity, these Founding Fathers of the Republic provided that "Congress shall make no law respecting an establishment of religion, or prohibiting the free exercise thereof." On the first clause rests the principle of church and state separation; on the second, our religious liberty. How far the second extends is being demonstrated these days by Jehovah's Witnesses. That frequently cantankerous millennial sect has carried a series of 46 cases to the Supreme Court, all bearing on the limits of religious liberty, and has won 39—a remarkable score, as any lawyer will tell you. As a result, we have today a much more plainly defined legal code covering the American conception of religious liberty than at any previous time. Some day someone will write a historic book on "The Contribution of Jehovah's Witnesses to Religious Freedom in the U.S.A."

As to the separation of church and state, I do not need to tell you how tense an issue that has suddenly become. This is the result of something referred to in Chapter 1—American Catholicism's change of outlook from that of a minority to that of a majority group. You can measure the change roughly by the fact that as recently as 1928, when Alfred E. Smith was running for president, he affirmed, in his memorable *Atlantic Monthly* article during that campaign, his complete acceptance of the separation of church and state, while five years ago another distinguished Catholic layman, at that time attorney general of the United States, J. Howard McGrath, in a speech at Cleveland not only declared that there is no constitutional basis for separation of church and state but insisted that there must not be even so much as a fence between them.

There are some Protestants who sympathize with the Catholic view to the extent of arguing that separation of church and state is such a vague concept, is so incapable of clear definition, that we had better not make too much of it. I do not believe this is so. The Supreme Court did not find it overly difficult to define the concept and lay down judicial orders based on such a definition in the most important modern decision bearing on this issue. The verdict in the McCollum case, you will recall, was 8 to 1, which indicates that there was not any large amount of confusion among the justices as to the principle involved. The concept that there is to be no interlocking of the official functions of the state

with the official functions of a church seems to me sufficiently clear to provide a rule susceptible to legal interpretation and undeviating observance. Such a rule does
not prohibit co-operation between church and state,
provided that each keeps its official functioning clear of
the other. But it does keep the wall of separation, of
which Jefferson wrote, plainly there. And I am convinced, on the basis of what is happening to public
school systems in some of our northern cities where the
Roman Catholic Church, with its contempt for the
principle of separation, has vast political influence, that
if we relax for a moment our vigilance to maintain this
principle in our national life, we shall thereby imperil
not only the Protestant position in America but the
foundations of the American democratic system.

One fruit of our traditional religious liberty has, of
course, been our denominational system. There have
been denominational divisions in other countries, but
nowhere else anything like the proliferation we have
seen here. Once we regarded this as a tribute to the
rugged individualism of the American; today we know
it is a scandal. To be sure, many of the 258 denominations listed in the census are mere splinter bodies of a
few hundred members, and the overwhelming majority
of American Protestants are to be found in about twenty
churches. But we know that even these divisions are too
many. They help to perpetuate a needless splitting up of
the Protestant forces—with consequent weakness—at
the local level, and they make the national impact of
Protestantism far less powerful than it should be. As a
result, the ecumenical spirit is working among us.

The federation movement has produced, since the
turn of the century, almost a thousand city, county, and
state federations of churches, a Federal Council of

Churches and other interdenominational agencies, and now a National Council of Churches. Although these bodies are no more than their names imply—councils, in which what the politicians would call fully sovereign denominations agree only to consult on mutual problems—nevertheless, in the background there is the hope that by meeting together and, whenever it is possible, working together, these denominations may eventually reach the point where they will be ready to give up some of their independent sovereignty and join together in full fellowship.

The other ecumenical path is, of course, that to outright union of churches. Dr. E. Stanley Jones believes that we could move forward along that path more rapidly than we are doing if we would be content to begin by making a great affirmation of union, leaving our local congregations and our denominational organizations as they now are, and then depending on the Spirit of God and the pressures of time to bring an acceleration of actual unions at the local and denominational level. It is hard to resist Dr. Jones' enthusiasm, and the response he evokes from laymen—including Episcopal and Lutheran laymen—is a matter of importance. But some of us still wonder whether what someone has called a "letterhead church union" will really come to grips with the problem of sectarian division which now so weakens the Protestant witness.

But church union, in the organic sense, is a hard goal to reach. There have been some unions, mostly of divided denominational families. The most arresting has, of course, been the union of Methodists, consummated in 1939. As for other unions, perhaps the most important have been those of the Congregational and Christian Churches (two congregational bodies) and of the

Evangelical and United Brethren Churches (two Methodist bodies). But unions across the lines of the historic traditions, such as those proposed between the Presbyterian and the Episcopal Churches, and between the Congregational-Christian and Evangelical and Reformed Churches, have either failed outright or are encountering very rough going. After a long delay in the courts the merger of the Congregationalists and Evangelical and Reformed, into what will be called the United Church of Christ is scheduled to be consummated in the near future.* It seems probable, however, that a considerable minority of Congregational Churches will refuse to enter the United Church.

Mention should be made of the so-called "Greenwich movement" to unite organically the Protestant denominations which recognize each other's sacraments and clerical orders. Representatives of eight or nine bodies, under the chairmanship of Methodist Bishop Ivan Lee Holt, put into definite form a proposed basis for union which this effort plans some day to place before these churches. The Greenwich movement does not seem likely, however, to become a major factor in American Protestant life for some years, if ever. If there were in this country the same general will to union in the divided ranks of Protestantism which brought into being the United Church of Canada, such a project as the formulation of the Greenwich plan would be of enormous immediate importance. But we might as well be candid and face the fact that there is no such will to union

* This merger was later legally consummated in 1956, making it possible for these churches in local communities to unite, but leaving the decision optional with the local churches. The first General Synod of the United Church of Christ is called for June 1957, at which time a constitution will be adopted.

here as our Canadian brethren have shown. While this remains the case, federation is about as far as we can go.

Other Aspects of American Protestant Life

There are a number of other aspects of American Protestant life which I should like to discuss if there were time and space. I should like to speak about the relation of our missionary enthusiasm—which has been so vital a factor in keeping up the spiritual vigor of our churches—to the new role of the United States as the outstanding world power. Already, the tensions inherent in America's competition with that other world power, communism, have forced the withdrawal of American missions from China, our largest mission field. Withdrawals may be forced in a few years from other fields. The outcry against "American imperialism" will not die down as long as it serves the purposes of the Communists to keep it going. And we need to realize that the enormous wealth of America makes this a poor base from which to project a Christian missionary enterprise to people who believe that it is not right that we should have so much while they have so little. It all makes the problem of the missionary future a delicate and nearly baffling one.

Something should probably be said about the theology of American Protestant churches today. I pass that subject by. There is an unmistakable revival of theological interest and emphasis, but the intellectual impulse and content for most of it has come from Europe. We have today few American theologians of importance. Niebuhr and Tillich come closest to that rank. Tillich is a refugee; and Niebuhr's thought has obvious European sources, though modified by American experience. Incidentally, since I am a Methodist myself, I should perhaps point out that there are no important Methodist theologians at present. Paul Ramsey probably comes closest to belonging in that category, and he has now transferred his teaching to Princeton Theological Seminary. Indeed, there may be food for reflection in the fact that if one were to name the five Methodist theological teachers of the active generation whose work is receiving most attention, all of them—Ramsey, Paul Minear, John Knox, Daniel D. Williams, and Georgia Harkness—are teaching in other than Methodist seminaries. And the one outstanding Methodist teacher of preaching, an art in which Protestantism stands in dire need, Halford E. Luccock, did his work in a nondenominational seminary.

Something, too, must be said about our race problem, intimately connected as that is with the future of churches in a nation that is being forced, by the inexorable demands of history, to play a role of global leadership. But I confess that on this problem I hardly know what can be said that will have any usefulness, for after we have talked all around and part-way through the race issue in our churches, where do we come out? We must admit that the problem is here, growing every day in complexity and in its inescapability.

We know that the race issue gains intensity from the collision between a rising generation of younger Negroes who have become intolerant of what they call the "Uncle Tom" race leadership of the past and a great number of whites who are resolute to resist all suggestions of change—and we know that we do not know the answer. We do not know the answer because our consciences and our New Testaments tell us that the answer should be of one sort, while our social *mores* tell us that it cannot be of that sort. But the implacable thrust of history makes it impossible for us to believe that we can long emulate the Roman governor Felix who, when faced by another baffling problem in which expediency warred with justice in the person of his prisoner, St. Paul, pushed it aside to wait for "a convenient season." This is one problem for which there will never be a convenient season.

The verdict of the Supreme Court on school segregation will make history far beyond the boundaries of the United States. Nothing has so weakened the efforts of this nation to commend to others its conception of democracy, or to establish a claim to world democratic leadership, as our ambiguous record on the race issue. Any American missionary can testify—and hundreds have done so—that no handicap he has encountered has had more damaging effect than the belief, widespread in Asia and Africa, that our national practices on race matters have been immoral and hypocritical.

I have no contribution to make to a solution; the longer I have moved around the southern states, the more I fear that the South has worked itself into a dilemma for which there is no solution this side of some sort of upheaval.

I have been struck by the contrast between church leaders on the race issue. The *Christian Century* of March 14, 1956, printed the horrifying comments of the pastor of the largest Southern Baptist church. Methodist bishops in the southeast, though quieter, are not much better. But I have encountered quite a number of Episcopal bishops who are outspoken against all segregation as sin, and the Southern Presbyterians are miles ahead of the Methodists and Baptists. What makes the difference? Is it the secure social prestige of the Episcopalians and Presbyterians?

When I mentioned the silence, or worse, of Methodist bishops in the South I should have added a tribute to those Methodist preachers who have sacrificed their careers to bear their witness to the demands of the gospel in this situation. There are quite a few of them, and they are good men. The Methodist "system" is a ladder-mounting affair, and if you provoke bishops and district superintendents you don't mount. Most of these men know they will not do much mounting for a long time, if ever. But prophecy is not dead within them, or in their pulpits.

The Methodist women, likewise, deserve recognition. They have not run to cover, as some "liberal" elements have, since the Supreme Court decision. They speak plainly, courageously, and persistently—and I have heard some of them speak disparagingly of the caution of their menfolk, especially in the episcopal ranks. When one remembers that the old justification for the segregation system was the need to protect southern womanhood, the decisive stand taken by these church-women is as amazing as it is heartening.

One thing that has interested and somewhat amused me is the bafflement of some Methodists and Baptists over what to do about the Roman Catholic stand on race. They know that the Catholic archbishop of St. Louis, a bishop in North Carolina, but most of all Archbishop Rummel of New Orleans, have run away with the ball so far as the churches are concerned—thinking in long-distance terms, that is. But what to do about it? They wish they knew.

I met a Sunday School teacher in a southern community who dared take an opinion poll in his adult class when there were more than 100 present. Result: unanimous agreement that segregation is anti-Christian and antidemocratic; unanimous agreement that integration inevitably is coming; nearly unanimous opinion that they would oppose its coming in their lifetime; majority opinion that they would hope it will not come in the lifetime of their children; less than half a dozen ready for integration now or any time. Secondary result: an appeal to the teacher to get back to "teaching the Bible."

On Good Friday, 1956, I attended an interracial service. The church was well filled on a hot afternoon; the Negro minister who preached on the sixth word from the cross brought the only meditation in that afternoon's series I remember. The service itself, held under the auspices of an integrated ministerial association, was a landmark in that southern town. It made me feel good —too good, for I suddenly realized that I was sitting submerged in self-righteous approval of myself for deigning to be present and listen to a true minister of Jesus Christ, by chance of birth with a darker skin than mine, preach a true gospel. And I fear that a good many others there felt the same pharisaical pride.

Hopes for the Future

What I have been saying does not, of course, affect the fact that we have hundreds of churches in our American Protestantism which are trying in every way they can to give moral guidance, hope, a sense of fellowship in the service of Christ to their members. Moreover, in these churches there is indisputable evidence that lives are being given direction, spirits sweetened, outlooks enlarged. We are even producing some saints— and I presume you can put that down as the ultimate test of the worth of a church—Protestant, Orthodox, Roman Catholic, Jehovah's Witnesses, Mormon, or what have you—its ability to produce saints. These things are so and, because they are so, we can thank God and take courage.

When we look to the future, we can expect most of these churches to go on rendering their inconspicuous but immeasurably important ministry to those who come within the radius of their influence. But what can we expect of American Protestantism in its larger aspects during the next decade or so? If the nation is not torn to pieces in a world conflict, so that every institution, including the churches, becomes absorbed in the stark problem, first, of survival, and then, of postsurvival recovery, it seems to me that a reasonable forecast would run along this line:

First, there will be a strengthening of ecumenical interest, much of it in terms of aid to churches and persons in devastated regions. I expect that our implication in the World Council of Churches is going to increase in proportion as we find ways through the Council of helping the needy in ravaged lands, rather than because of anything the Council may contribute to our thinking on theological and ecclesiastical issues on which there will be talk and talk and talk without getting anywhere. Here is the general line of advance, I believe, by which our missionary movement may be refitted to the necessities of this day. If, perchance, working not in denominational separateness but through the National Council and the World Council, and in co-operation not with just our own government but with the United Nations—which can hardly be charged with imperialism—we can find the ways to do what needs to be done to succor the afflicted in devastated and undernourished portions of the earth, and to assist them to a life filled with hope for tomorrow—if we could do this, we could quickly re-

gain our missionary spirit and our ecumenical loyalty
would take on substance and power.

Second, I trust that during these next ten or twenty
years the movement for union of the Protestant churches
will move ahead. I think that for the present, the best
results are to be hoped for if these efforts concentrate
largely on reunions with main groups of churches. But
"the wind bloweth where it listeth," and it may be that
opportunities for other unions, reaching across traditional boundaries, will appear. I believe, however, that
we can expect most from development of the federative
principle and spirit, and that this has much more to
contribute to the ultimate extinction of the scandal of
a divided Protestantism than we have so far discovered.

Third, during these next few decades I hope American Protestantism will take the lead in putting the study
of religious lore back into the American public school
system. Note what I say: not the study of religion, but
the study of religious lore. To attempt the first would be
further to divide our American communities and to
strike a terrible blow at the principle of separation of
church and state. But the lore of religion is a fundamental element in culture, and no student will come out of
our schools with a fully rounded basic education who is
ignorant in this regard. There is nothing, either in law
or in principle, to keep the public schools—and in this
I include the high schools and state and city universities
—from teaching the lore of religion. The thing that is
preventing it is inertia in the school system, and the
covert opposition of certain elements which like to
point to the absence of religious lore from the public
school curriculum as proof of the need for a parallel
parochial school system. It is Protestantism's responsi-

bility to end that inertia in the school system, and I trust that before long it will move to do so.

Fourth, I also have a hope that in the years just ahead we may see within American Protestantism a lay awakening something like that which forms such an element of promise in postwar Continental Protestantism. Here, I believe, is about our only chance to re-establish friendship with the developing labor movement. At the moment, the Roman Catholic Church, with its labor schools studying the social encyclicals of recent popes and its Association of Catholic Trade Unionists, is far ahead of Protestantism in this regard. But this is a clerically directed movement, as all Catholic movements turn out to be. In the long run, a powerful trade union movement in this country is not going to take its direction from any clerical source, however high-minded. A lay revival in Protestantism, provided it takes in more than the owners and managers of industry and the white-collar group, might really get somewhere in struggling for the soul of American labor.

Moreover, I hope that such a lay revival, if it should come, would take some of the emphasis off institutionalism which, it seems to me, has gone to excessive lengths in American Protestantism. I am not adverse to seeing great Protestant cathedrals springing up all over the country, and new buildings on the campuses of hard-pressed Protestant colleges. But the plant is not everything. It is the spirit and the personalities within the plant which count. Not long ago I heard a religious education leader say that in his long experience he had known many churches to raise large sums to expand their religious education plants, but he had never known one to do the same thing to expand its staff. As long as a church has a director of religious education, it seems to be satisfied. From that point on, all it is interested in is more plant. The same fault appears in other parts of Protestant church life. I hope that we are heading toward a lay revival, and that when it comes it will take some of the emphasis off plant expansion and put it on service through deeply concerned personalities.

So I come to the end of this effort to examine the part which the Christian churches are playing in the crisis of these times and the part which they may be expected to play in the years immediately ahead. There is, it seems to me, no cause for complacency in our present situation, and no cause for despair. What we need most of all is a new sense of the greatness, the marvel, of our gospel and of the desperate need of men and nations. If the first ever takes hold on us, the second will follow. And when the second follows, our ministries will be freed from their parochialism, from the temptation to become absorbed in matters of minor moment—both of them conditions which are so often the source of discouragement.

What I have been saying within this book has had behind it a hope that it may help Christians to see the gravity of the position in which the church finds itself at this hour. It has not, however, been brought forward as a cause for discouragement. Complacency, a superficial optimism, contentment with the traditional and the routine—these are states of mind we need to get rid of, but we have no reason to lose courage. We have a gospel which is the Word of Life. We have a Lord and Master who is the answer to men's needs. We have a fighting chance. What more can we ask?